GROWING WILD

Answering the call to rise
while staying rooted in love

BY KATHRYN VIGNESS

Book design, layout, and formatting by Amber Hargett

ISBN: 978-0-692-17552-1 (Paperback)

First Edition

TABLE OF CONTENTS

for mark,
from one free bird to another,
thank you for showing me how to soar.

INTRODUCTION

Well, here we are. This is the part where I write a witty letter to impart some grandiose wisdom and guidance for you as you embark on this story. Let's just throw the obvious out there and say, never in a million years did I think that I would be writing a book.

Actually, retract that. I always knew I'd write a book, but never in a million years did I think I was going to be writing about me, about my life. Let's just say I envisioned that I would write some educational, self-help book that assisted in discovering one of the secrets to living a joy-filled life. And I would write it years down the road after I retired when I had the time to check things off my bucket list. Maybe by that time I would've experienced enough through my life lessons, travel, and meeting people that I would eventually learn that secret to pass on to others.

But that's the thing about having plans. What's that saying? *If you want to hear God laugh, tell Him your plans*. Right? It's never up to us. God always has the bigger plan for our lives. There is no other time than now; the lessons and journey that I've been through have all led up to this.

Every time I tried to outline a book, all of the lessons I wanted to share, it ultimately led me back to here. At the beginning. I couldn't move forward until I acknowledged and healed the past. I wrote this book for a number of reasons. First, and most obvious, being a published author is a total bucket list item. But more than that, I wanted to let go of the stories I identified myself with. You will read about how my healing didn't start until as of late, even when tragedy struck me early on in life.

As a life coach and speaker, I am hired to show up authentically, yet deep inside, I felt like such a fraud. I was a shapeshifter; morphing into who the client needed me to be. There was a seismic disconnect because I preached about living an intentional and authentic life, yet here I was, never taking my own advice. The kicker is I have done it most of my life, this shapeshifting. Morphing into the roles and archetypes I thought I was supposed to be; believing the stories and limiting beliefs I told myself.

The various roles and archetypes I created slowly cracked and eventually crumbled because I never fixed the foundation: the story in which made me. It took me writing this book to realize that I am not my story. These stories were the breakdowns, which ultimately led me to the breakthroughs. If I continued to run from the past, I could never honor the lives that influenced me and made me who I am today. Because my path has a greater purpose than myself. All the fires I lived through gave me the opportunity to rise time and time again. I found my strength among the ashes, where vulnerability is the secret ingredient to growth.

Above all, I wrote this book because at the end of my life, I want to be able to proudly say, *I have used all of my gifts, I come completely empty. All the storms I've weathered, I understand they were placed along my path to learn how to strengthen my roots and still reach for the stars. Thank you for using me as a vessel so that I could pour into those around me. And if given the chance to relive this life all over again, I wouldn't change a single thing.*

I am finally ready to share all of me with all of you. Intentionally. Authentically. My hope is that a piece of my story resonates with you, that you see your reflection in my words and know you are not alone in the struggles that we call share: the stories we believe are holding us back. The shame and unworthiness and insignificance of our lives. The struggle to keep putting one foot in front of the other because we have no idea where we're headed. The second-guessing after we change our mind. The inability to find that one thing as a passion, but rather be passionate about many things. The beauty of wearing our hearts on our sleeves and raising babies that do the exact same.

My prayer is that my story gives you the courage to answer the call to rise while staying rooted in love. Because we can't fly without having somewhere to land.

"Like a wild flower;
She spent her days,
Allowing herself to grow,
Not many knew of her struggle,
But eventually all; knew of her light."

– Nikki Rowe

chapter one
....

THE MIGHTY OAK

When I was a little girl, nothing was off limits. I grew up wild in the Red River Valley alongside my two brothers, free to roam throughout the fields and woods between my family's house and farm in rural Northwest Minnesota. I would spend hours wandering in and out of culverts, building tree forts with old plywood, splashing and swimming through the coulee, and creating a collection of rocks along the way. Never once did I get lost in the thick woods, as my internal compass always pointed me home.

By the time I was 10, around 1994, my brothers Matt and Mark, ages 18 and 14 respectively, were old enough to be in sports and hang out with their friends or were working with my dad in the fields, so I found myself alone regularly during the summer and into fall. Minnesota in the fall was a perfect time with the leaves changing and the Northern Lights to dance at night. I found peace and solstice being outside with my dog, Ginger. She was the quintessential farm dog as a black lab with some German Shepherd and retriever mix. Her dark fur was coarse and thick with tan markings down her back and legs. Ginger was my companion, a true best friend. I told her all of my stories, and she was my sidekick on all of my adventures, reciprocated with wet, slobbery kisses. She always loved a good chest rub.

One cool fall day, I crunched through the woods with Ginger at my side. In front of us squirrels scurried up the trees while rabbits darted off for cover in the thicket. I could hear the geese flying south while magpies squawked at me from atop of the trees. In my mind, the wildlife was my audience, and I, the center of attention. For every one of my imaginary productions, I used odd shaped sticks and rocks as my props, along with other random treasures I found along the way.

"Ginger," I started talking as I laid back on a clearing at the edge of the coulee. I placed my arm behind my head and felt the cold, damp earth support me as I gazed up at the sky. "Suppose one day when I'm big and famous and on Broadway, do you think I'll still be able to see the stars at night?" I longed for depth and expansiveness, much like the fields and skies on the Great Plains where you could see for miles and miles. I longed for a something more, although I didn't know what that was.

Even though I was a major tomboy, I wasn't much help on the farm, as the hog feeders were automated and picking rock in the fields was only a springtime task. Besides, that's the perk of having older brothers...I wasn't my dad's first go-to when it came to farm help. Even when it came to Barbie dolls or princesses, I wasn't your typical girl. I always found myself daydreaming about brave, empowered heroines. In any fairytale or Disney story, I truly loved when the girl went after what she wanted. She followed her heart, all while demonstrating courage and kindness along the way.

For a few moments I laid there, watching the Indian summer sun dart behind the trees that were gently blowing in the breeze. I watched as some of the leaves that had already turned vibrant colors of reds, oranges, and yellow release and flutter to the ground around me. Still thinking out loud, I said to her, "I bet I will. I mean, no matter where I am, I'll always be able to look at the stars and feel like I'm home." Ginger was sniffing her way around me and finally sat down next beside me, impatient to keep going. "Okay, we'll go to the tree!"

We continued on our walk toward what I called, "The Mighty

Oak". This tree was like a magnet for me, as no matter where I would roam, I always found myself ending up there. With over a 25ft circumference, when I hugged the tree, my lanky arms barely covered any area. I often found myself climbing over the exposed roots that resembled Medusa as they were spindled around each other, snaking in and out of the ground all around the tree. I would balance as I walked and jumped from limb to limb, as if it were a dance that only I knew. In this tree was the first time that I felt my imagination come to life. I came to her with my hopes and my dreams, somehow knowing I could receive the answers she held. In any of my outdoor adventures, I always knew I could find myself a place of rest in those roots, being connected deep to the earth and still feel supported in my dreams and ambitions as I looked up at the limitless sky.

"What do I need to know today?" I whispered, sitting on a limb. In the distance through the trees, I could see the dust flying up all the way down the gravel road behind Matt's 1984 silver Chevy Nova as he was just getting back from football practice. Slowly pulling into the drive right behind him was my Dad and brother Mark coming back from the farm doing chores.

Ginger and I sprinted toward the house with the wind at our backs.

• • •

As I joined my family in the house to wash and shower up for supper, something marvelous greeted me: the sound of the electric beaters whipping the mashed potatoes, and the sight of my mom in her red apron finishing up the last of the sides for the meal. After washing my hands, my stomach growled as I sat down in my usual spot at the already set table.

"We have to leave by 6:30 for Mass tonight, so make sure that you're all ready to go," my mom Gay, said as she placed the mashed potatoes onto the table. Nobody responded as we already knew and to be honest, we were more concerned about eating than giving up a weeknight for church. Meals were a focal point in our family, as my mom loved to cook and host and the rest of us loved to eat, as we had good Scandinavian hearty appetites. Typically, Sunday dinner after Mass was our big meal, yet most days of the week we had large family suppers, too. "Your grandmother wants to go out to Bergeson's this weekend, so I'm going to take her," my mom announced as she placed the potatoes on the table. "Mark, when we get home tonight, be sure to clean up your mess outside."

"Mmmhhmm," Mark replied.

"Kathryn, I spoke with your teacher this afternoon," my mom started.

"Oooh!" both brothers sneered as they dropped their forks and smirked across the table at me. "Sister's in *trouble*!" Mark teased with a big goofy grin on his face. I shot him a glare back.

"Boys," my mom tried to silence them. "She is not in trouble! Mind your own business, as I can surely talk to your teachers if I need to, too!" That quieted them right up, but they still snickered silently at me. My mom was a beloved teacher in our small K-12 school and it seemed as if she had eyes and ears everywhere there, as she knew everything that went on. "Anyway," my mom continued, "It seems as if you and Lauren seem to be adding in a lot of extra commentary to the classroom." I just rolled my eyes and picked up my fork again to keep eating. "Well, it's just the beginning of the year and already we have a problem. Let's see if we can focus a bit more on school and not so much socializing, okay?"

"But, Mom!" I dejectedly replied. "It's not just me talking! It's everyone. I'm just the one who is talking when Mrs. Norris asks us to stop!"

"Sister's got a big mouth!" Mark teased to Matt quietly, but just loud enough for me to hear.

"Shut up!" I yelled across the table pointedly.

"Kathryn, that's enough," said my mom.

"How do I get in trouble when he's being the snot?" I asked defiantly, dropping my fork on my plate which made a loud ting. I kept my eyes on Mark who was smirking as he quietly ate, surely soaking in my trouble versus his.

"Mark, be done." My mom changed the subject. "Kathryn, do you want to go with me out to Bergeson's?"

I had just gotten back to my meal. Like a wild animal, too engrossed in my food, I just shrugged without looking up. Everyone else at the table apparently was just as hungry as I was, since there were second helpings of food passed more than conversation flowing.
Leaning back in his chair, Mark tried to get my attention. "Sister," he said, calling me my kid nickname. "Wanna play go get-em when we get home tonight? If you help me clean up, we can play." Always trying to weasel his way out of his chores, Mark knew that instigating me with my favorite game would surely enlist my help, especially after teasing me so bad.

"Okay!" I replied, seemingly forgetful of what just transpired. I was always up for a game of go get-em. It was basically a glorified fielding practice. My dad or Matt hit fly balls to Mark and he'd throw them back and you guessed it, I'd go and get them to hand back to hit. (Not as if I was an imperative part of practice, but anytime my brothers wanted to play, I was more than ready.)

"Dad? You in?" asked Mark.

"Sure, we can do that," my dad replied. "But we have to go and check on the hogs first. We need to make sure they'll have enough water for the night."

We excused ourselves from the table, one by one, as soon as we finished eating. Calling me back, my mom asked, "Kathryn, will you clear the rest of the table, please?" I dutifully turned around and started stacking up the plates and brought them to the kitchen where she stood by the sink washing dishes. "Thank you, babe. I don't want to be late for Mass."

• • •

The car ride into Fertile was a quick 15 minute one, with my dad driving, my mom in the passenger seat, and I was sandwiched in between my brothers. Our car rides were characteristically quiet, except for my mom asking questions or Mark bugging me.

"Is church long tonight?" moaned Mark from the backseat.

"No, it'll be quick," replied my mom.

"So why do we have to go?" Mark protested.

"It's a holy day of obligation," she said. "And I don't want to hear any more fuss about it. You knew all week we were going. Matt, you're an altar server, you know."

"Ugh," he groaned. Since we were thick in the midst of adolescence, the level of teenage attitude was amplified, and responses from my brothers resembled more like caveman grunts more than words.

We were a very traditional, nuclear family with conservative parents, all while raising their kids to be the same. As the youngest, I could already see the different dynamics of adolescence and adulthood. My dad Greg, was very reserved and stoic, dressed in his cotton button down and khaki dress pants. My mom was in a floral dress with pearls, hair gracefully sprayed into place in her short pixie cut. Then there were us kids in the back, wearing jeans and either a sweatshirt or tee that had a '90s logo like B.U.M. or sporting our high school sports team plastered across the front. As long as it was clean, didn't have any holes in it, and was not borderline vulgar (as Matt tried to get away with sometimes) my mom didn't pick fights over what we wore.

She may have questioned it as, "Are you going to be wearing *that*?" hoping we would realize it wasn't her first choice of an outfit but didn't make it into something to argue about to make us late. To complete my tomboy look, I had an unkempt ponytail with what was left of my perm curling the ends, and cockeyed glasses which framed my face, as the nosepiece broke off after wrestling with Mark months before. I didn't care; I was one of the boys.

As we filed into our pew at church, a good ten minutes early, Mark and I shuffled in our spots while Matt found his way to the sacristy. Much like cattle, everyone in our small church had their stalls, or pews, if you will. The Ricards sat right up front, the Ericksons were kiddy-corner from us, and my family was halfway up the aisle. Mark was one who always thought it was an opportune time to get a laugh...for him or others. So naturally, his 14-year-old self made sure to sit right next to me. Once Mass started, Mark had already begun singing off key on purpose, and by the second reading, he had his arms crossed and was covertly flicking me in the arm, progressively getting stronger.

"Stop it!" I whispered loudly, scooting over ever so slightly to get away, only to be met by his sly grin as he scooted closer with me. We stood for the reading of the Gospel so, he stopped; only to start up again as we sat for the Homily. The instigator that he was, he knew that he could get a rise out of me by wearing me down. He didn't have to say a word, just be persistent in his pursuit of annoying me. "Knock it off," I growled more intensely, pulling my arm away, trapped between him and my mom. She looked over and down at me with eyes that meant that I needed to knock it off, as she didn't realize what Mark was doing. We were distracting her from the Lord's Word, and that was not something to be taken lightly.

Yet, he persisted. Mark continued with an irregular consistency that drove me batty. My fuse short, I couldn't take it any longer. One last flick and I raised my fist and slammed it down on his thigh hard enough to make him jump as he gave a muffled cry. Of course, that was the last straw for my mom as she leaned into both of us and said calmly, with a slight fierceness in her tone, "You two better knock it off right now. We are in church, and you will sit here quietly." She then wrapped her arm around me and pulled me in, as if to protect me from whatever Mark was about to do next.

Our family always held hands to say the Lord's Prayer, so I braced myself as I knew Mark would try to squeeze it as hard as he could, so I would wince in pain. When it was time for the Peace Offering, we stood to shake hands and again, Mark shook my hand feverishly, so I would laugh. He did it to almost everyone, besides my parents, of course. The socialite in me loved giving Peace as I was finally free to move, turn around and say hello to everyone and shake hands; the one part in Mass where I didn't have to sit still and be quiet. My excitement almost bubbled over as I shook hands with practically everyone, leaning across my parents or pews to connect.

"That's more than enough now Kathryn," my mom said quietly as she placed her hands on my shoulders and turned me back around to the front where the painfully shy boy from my Sunday School class was sitting in the pew in front of me.

"Peace be with you, Kathryn," he said, sticking his hand out but trying not to look me in the eyes.

"Peace, Aaron," I replied as I held out my hand and continued down the line of his family. As Mass ended and we were walking out of the church, my parents greeted and chatted with the other parishioners as my brothers and I hung out with our friends. As the only Catholic Church in our small community, we had a handful of classmates to connect with, trying to pass the time until our parents were done chatting and we could go home. Fellowship after church was lost on adolescents.

On the car ride home, I found myself looking out the window at the changing landscape, clouds, and impending sunset, mesmerized at the expansiveness of God's creation. I often found myself in the back seat, daydreaming as I tried to out drown out my parent's chatter, the crooning of country music on the radio, and ignoring Mark's annoying attempts to get a rise out of me. I frequently escaped reality and created a new world where dumb brothers weren't the focal point in, and I wasn't too much for others.

"Kathryn! Are you listening?" I jolted out of my zone to hear my mom questioning me.

"Huh?" I asked again.

"I asked if you are going to school early with me or riding the bus tomorrow?" my mom asked again, slightly irritated.

"Oh, yeah. I'll go with you," I replied ignoring the rest of what she was saying and going back to the scene out my window just waiting until I could get home and play outside for the remainder of the night. As we drove into the yard, I couldn't wait to get out of the backseat of that car. My mom always saw me as her little sidekick that was willing to follow, and I loved going on errands with her, but it wasn't easy to confide in her. She brushed hard topics and conversations under the rug. "How much longer before bed?" I asked as I bent down to greet Ginger.

"You have 45 minutes," my mom replied as she walked into the house. "Don't be getting all dirty playing, though. You already had a shower."

"Yep," I haphazardly replied as I took off for the woods, eager to get back to my daydream. As I made my way back through the woods, I noticed how significantly cooler it was now that the sun had started to go down. I stayed along the coulee, so I could stay in the sun and its warmth. "Too much commentary," I muttered as I walked, rethinking of what my mom said at supper.

It was a frequent comment I've heard at almost every parent-teacher Conference. *"Kathryn is a great student, but she likes to talk. Her grades show great improvement, but we've had to separate her from her friends because she likes to visit a little too much."* Or the fact that I wasn't invited to my friend's birthday party because they were going to do some Fall crafts and her mom didn't trust me with scissors as I was known to go overboard with projects. Or at least that's what my 10-year-old friend relayed to me.

"Too much is what I always hear," I grumbled some more as I kept walking, keeping my face to the sunshine. I stopped up ahead and watched the sun fade behind the grain elevator in Beltrami. I soaked in the last of the warmth on my face but witnessed the magnificent bursts of orange, red, and yellow that lit up the clouds and sky. "Maybe I'm not too much," I thought out loud, watching the sunset. "Maybe I just haven't shown all my colors yet." I watched the sky shift and change before my eyes. "No, I'm not too much. My colors are just too bright for everyone else."

And as I watched the last of the sun went down, I turned back around and raced past the Mighty Oak and through the field back home. I felt the tree's energy calling to me as if to reassure me that everything would be okay. Knowing full well that I needed to find solstice in her roots and to dream among her branches, breathing life into the beautiful growth that was undoubtedly to come.

chapter two

....

ROOTED

The following year, energy was high and magnetic as we were hurrying around the house after we got home from church. It was a flurry of activity before we had to leave bright and early to get a good seat in the crowded gymnasium to watch Matt walk across the stage and get his diploma. By the time Louise, my old babysitter got there, I was in full-on defiant mode.

"But Moooooom! I don't want to sit there for that long!" I pleaded.

"Kathryn, your brother is graduating. You will be there," she replied, exasperated.

"Why can't I stay with Louise? I can help!"

"Kathryn! I'm not going to argue about this anymore. You are going. End of conversation," my mom said as she walked out of the kitchen to finish putting on her jewelry and put one last spritz in her hair.

"UGH. Why can't I stay here?" I whined to myself as I organized the plates and napkins. Tending to everything, knowing it had to be just right for the smorgasbord of food for the party, I did not realize Louise was listening.

"Your mom wants things to be perfect. Remember, it's a big

17

day for her, too," Louise offered quietly. Louise always knew how to defuse tensions with me. She should, as our trusty babysitter and my second mom; she had watched my brothers and I since Matt was a baby.

As my mom breezed back into the kitchen, her long navy dress flowing and bracelets dangling, she stopped to take another look at me: glasses still askew on my untouched face, frizzy hair from being freshly washed, a long floral pink dress that cinched in the back, and dirty feet from running outside with the dog to pass the time until we had to go.

"Is it okay that she says here?" my mom confirmed with Louise.

"Absolutely. I'll put her to work, and we will have everything ready by the time you get back," replied Louise. "Go. Take lots of pictures, and we'll see you when you get back."

My mom sighed one more time, surely a sign of defeat that she didn't want to argue with me anymore. The last thing she wanted was to have me ruin a big day for Matt...or her. As extended family kept arriving to the house, I was thankful for the energetic reprieve as I greeted everyone at the door. My dad and brothers dressed in button-down shirts and ties, came out to mingle as well. Matt flung his sport coat over the recliner, as a reminder to grab it before heading out the door later.

I avoided eye contact with my mom, knowing how important of a day this was for her, I'm sure she was slightly relieved not to have to put up with my attitude. In her eyes, my absence vastly outweighed having my pouting ruin her ideal picture of the whole family celebrating Matt's momentous occasion. Something inevitably lost on my defiant 11-year-old spirit.

One by one, the cars backed out of the driveway, and the trail of dust lingered after the last car turned onto the highway. I turned and looked at Louise, to which she handed me a stack of plates.

18

"Alright, Katrink," she said, calling me by her favored nickname for me. "Let's get to work."

• • •

As a testament of how well-loved Matt was, our house flooded with people. By the time the party was in full swing, I was bopping in and out of the house, politely greeting friends and family, yet careful not to get trapped in a boring adult conversation that I was surprisingly good at. As an old soul, I loved connecting with my mom's older friends who enjoyed chatting with a bright-eyed, young kid. I loved getting lost in their stories of growing up, lessons learned, and ultimately profound wisdom that they passed down on me. I ate it up, too, as I always found myself asking more questions, never ready to go home quite yet. Small talk, on the other hand, made my eyes glaze over. And in a rural farming community, weather and small-town gossip were the two primary sources of chatter; a juxtaposition of elements well out of the talker's control.

For me, there was a mix of wanting to be seen and wanting to find solstice by disappearing into the woods with my dog; I felt like I was an imposter. Showing up physically, and yet not authentically. Fully understanding that the day was not about me, I wondered if anyone would even know if I slipped off on my own. Something I would question for much of my life.

As I was scooping up another handful of table mints, my absolute favorite, my mom stopped me. "Can you go get Matt? Your grandmother wants to get a picture of him with his quilt," she said. Without saying a word, I tossed a few mints into my mouth, spun around on my heel and walked past the ornate display with Matt's face in every picture and out the door. Passing my dad lost in conversation with family, I found Matt outside talking with his baseball coach and approached him.

"Mafoo, Mom wants you," I interrupted, inadvertently calling him by the one nickname he hated—the name I've called him since I was a toddler, not able to say Matthew. It was a habit hard to break even though he insisted I try.

"What?" he snapped, clearly annoyed.

"Mom wants a picture with your quilt," I recited, annoyed right back that I was just the messenger. Matt just rolled his eyes and told me he would be in in a minute.

I saw my classmate, Lauren, pulling into the drive, so instead of relaying back his message to my mom, I waved as I walked over and greeted her with a smile as she got out of the car. "Come on! Let's go in and get some punch! It has ice cream in it!" I exclaimed as I pulled her arm towards the house. Thankful to have someone my age to talk to, we weaved our way around others with full plates and cups. "Oh my gosh! Did you see what Templeton wrote in my yearbook? She actually thought we were friends," I laughed, then changed into a sarcastic tone. "Uh, no. I was just stuck with her for a math partner all year!"

As a creative bully, I talked big, but was never fully outwardly mean to people; instead I was very much catty behind their backs. I craved attention—even negative attention from the teacher. Being the creative I was, it was right up my alley to find some tick in a classmate and mercilessly taunt them about it. For example, Templeton. She was a classmate who had a short, pixie haircut, only with a rat tail, as was very popular in the '90s. Instead of calling her Rat and having her know I was talking about her, I called her Templeton, because that was the rat's name in my favorite book, *Charlotte's Web*.

Giggling together as we neared food line, my mom stopped us. "Hello, Lauren!" she said smiling, then turned to me. "Did you get Matt?"

"I told him, and he said it'll be just a minute," I said as we made our way through the food line.

"Well, that was more than five minutes ago," she replied, stressed that things were not on her schedule. A calm wave washed over her face as she peered out the window looking for him. "Oh there he is, talking to Bob. Your grandmother is waiting."

Matt must have known that he had extended his so-called minute long enough, and sauntered in through the front door, putting his suit coat back on and adjusting his tie. My mom beamed as he approached, and she purposefully got my grandparents' attention. Standing in front of the hallway, next to the guestbook and photo-adorned table, and behind the custom-made navy patchwork quilt hanging elegantly on the quilt rack, Matt stood in between my grandparents who gifted it to him.

"Smile, everyone!" my mom tried, knowing full well that Matt was very sparse with his smiles, especially after all of the other photos taken earlier. Louise snapped the picture, as she was the queen of capturing all of our big moments growing up, a huge relief to my mom as remembering to take pictures was not her strong suit.

Grumbling and loosening his tie, Matt asked, "Are we done with pictures, yet?"

"Yes, Matt. You are done," replied my mom, permitting him to change out of the dress clothes he so loathed wearing.

Blocking the door to the basement where Matt so desperately wanted to retreat to, Uncle Kent shook Matt's hand and started in. "So, UMC and baseball, huh?"

"Yep," replied Matt.

"I loved my college playing days," reminisced Kent, who played four seasons of college baseball himself. "U of M is a great school to play for and a great education. You won't regret going there." Matt just nodded, agreeing; yet trying to acknowledge a way to move past Kent and change in peace and quiet. Just then Lauren and I snuck past and squeezed through the small opening of the basement door, and I locked eyes with Matt.

"Excuse me," Matt said, motioning towards me in the door behind Kent.

"Oh, sorry!" said Kent, moving out of the way. Thinking he would find refuge in the basement, Matt came down the stairs to find Lauren and, I sprawled out on the couch, turning on the TV. Mark heard the commotion and left his room, also located in the basement, to see what was going on.

"This sucks," Matt said, clearly over the grandiose attention and small talk with everyone who came to congratulate him. "I can't wait to get out of here."

"Me either!" quipped Mark.

"No, like for good. I'm so over this small-town shit," explained Matt as he kept walking to his room.

As Lauren flipped through the channels, I couldn't help but wonder what Matt meant about what he said. I felt conflicted, knowing full well my heart and soul were meant for big things, and yet I loved the small, tight-knit community that made me feel safe. I was happy. Everything was just right, with our whole family together. Matt moving out and going to college was the first step in growing pains that I would experience. I didn't realize how full of conflicting emotions I was of where life would take me. Little did I know what a journey would unfold.

• • •

Sixth grade was a mixed bag of hormones, catty friendships, and I was still very much a tomboy, yet I secretly hoped a cute boy would see past the acne, broken glasses, and awful haircut. I wanted to believe in a happily ever after and I was sure that underneath all of the ugly, a beautiful swan was waiting to emerge. Only, she hadn't.

There was one boy who wouldn't leave me alone, however. I was forced to be partners with him on class projects as I was a "model student"...except for the fact that I still talked too much in class. Harry had a crush on me, and the whole class knew it. But instead of showing affection, Harry did quite the opposite. He teased and mocked me, which in turn, made me retaliate right back out of spite to show him how much I did *not* like him. Growing up with two brothers, I am no match when it comes to mercilessly teasing; my skin is thick, and I have a hot temper. I was also a one-upper, meaning I always had to have the last zinger. It was my prerogative.

One day, however, things escalated very quickly between Harry and me. Lauren and I were walking down the stairs to lunch, when I heard a boy calling my name.

"Hey, Kathryn." I turned, and as I did, I felt a thwap on my head. In front of me was Harry with a huge, round rainbow lollipop in his hand and he was laughing.

"What the hell did you do that for?" I demanded, outraged.

"Ha!" Harry laughed, eyes twinkling. "Got you!" And just as fast as he came, he ran down the steps two at a time to get in line for lunch. I rubbed my sore head and continued down after him.

Still seething as I ate my lunch, I thought of all the ways I could hurt that dumb Harry Voll. I could hardly concentrate on eating or the conversations between friends, because I kept looking through them to the table kiddie-corner to Harry, glaring. He was oblivious to my rage and continued to eat his mashed potatoes and turkey gravy. I secretly thought of picking up my lump of potatoes and throwing it at his face, but he was too far across the lunchroom, and I did not want to be responsible for a food fight. I remember how much trouble the boys in the other class got for flinging their mashed potatoes at the ceiling to make them stick. We headed out to the playground for recess and Harry was hiding, waiting for me behind some playground equipment.

"Hey Kathryn," he taunted as I walked by. "Want a treat?"

I looked over at him, and he was waving the same lollipop at me. Rage boiled within my veins. I stormed over to him, ready to let him have it.

"What the hell's wrong with you?" I shouted. "What gives you the right to hit me with that thing?" I hit his hand and knocked the sucker to the ground. I got in his face and growled, "If you know what's good for you, you will walk away now."

Instead of taking my advice, Harry laughed in my face. "What are you gonna do about it, hit me?"

At this time, our playground attendant walked up to us, "Whoa, whoa! What's all this commotion about, kids?" Her crooked smile had a way of diffusing situations, and I backed up to gain some distance between the three of us.

"*He* hit me on the head with that sucker!" I yelled, pointing to the ground where it still lay.

"Is that true?" she asked Harry.

"Well, yeah..." he trailed off, but I saw a trace of a sneer come across his face. "But she said she wants to hit *me*!" as he pointed at me.

"Is that true?" she asked as she turned to me.

"Yeah, because he deserves it!" I shouted indignantly at Harry. By this time, a small crowd had gathered because of all the commotion.

"Okay," the playground attendant said, taking a step back. "Hit him."

I stood there shocked. This was not the first scuffle Harry and I had been in, but that was not the answer or solution I anticipated.

"Wait, what?" I said.

"Hit him," she repeated, calling my bluff.

"I don't throw the first punch," I replied cockily.

So, she turned to Harry, "Okay, you hit her."

"Oh, right. Like I'm going to punch a *girl*," he sneered, which made my blood boil once again. The way he made the word girl sound made it seem as if he was so much better off than I.

"You scared?" I taunted. "Come on! Do it. What? Are you afraid of a girl?"

"No," he said, trying to justify himself. "I'm not gonna hit you. You don't hit girls."

By this time, an even bigger crowd had emerged to watch. Loving the attention, I didn't stop. "Figures as much. You can only hit girls over the head with a sucker behind their back, huh? I knew you couldn't do anything to my face!"

I lunged forward, "C'mon! Hit me!" I screamed. I was so close to his face I could still smell his lunch on his breath.

Harry took a step back and pretended to punch me over my

shoulder, his arm as limp as a noodle. "There, you happy?"

I looked at the playground attendant and asked, "Does that count?"

She laughed and said, "Sure." Before she knew it, my fist connected with Harry's face and he was on the ground holding it. The playground attendant was stunned, and it took a second for her to realize what happened and knelt down to Harry. He pinched his nose with his fingers and looked up at her with blood dripping down. "Kathryn, Principal's office! Right now!" she yelled as the kids in the crowd dispersed when they saw it was trouble. "Harry, come with me," as she escorted him off the playground and to the nurse.

Next, I found myself inside the elementary principal's office all alone, staring at the old class composites hanging on the wall. He had left to get my mom from her classroom down the hall and have a talk with me. The bell rang, and I could hear the slamming of locker doors and rustling of students getting to their next class.

"Pssst!" I turned and saw Mark's bright eyes and big smile peering through the doorway. "Is it true?" he asked.

"What?" I asked, pretending not to know what he was talking about.

"Sister," he said annoyingly. "Is it true?"

I caved and smiled. "Yeah."

"Did you throw the first punch?" he asked.

"Nope," I replied matter-of-factly.

His smile grew even bigger. "Atta, girl!" he said and disappeared as fast as he came, knowing full well not to get caught by the principal or mom.

. . .

When I was in seventh grade, I finally had my very first boyfriend. At 12, I was dating Josh, a 15-year-old boy from another school, for a few months. I loved the thought of dating someone who didn't know me. It made me feel special to have someone ask me questions of my family and friends, my dreams, and my interests instead of picking a boy from my hometown who I've known since Kindergarten and practically related to them all. The first time I met Rick, Josh's friend, he put me in my place.

"Hi, I'm Kathryn," I introduced myself.

"What's your name?" Rick asked, squinting his eyes and cocking his head as I was speaking a foreign language.

"My name is Kathryn," I repeated, slower this time, unsure where this was going.

He paused for a moment. "Well that's the stupidest name I've ever heard," he replied, rolling his eyes and starting to walk away. "I'm not gonna call you that. I'm just gonna call you Kat."

That defining moment became a fixture ingrained in my memory. Even my name wasn't good enough for this round, pimple-laden, pre-pubescent 15-year-old boy. I stood horrified while Rick and Josh laughed; my first boyfriend and his friend blatantly dismissed me.

And while the fire burned within me of someone being so disrespectful to me, I just stood there, silently dying inside. For the first time, I put on a mask known as Kat to protect my heart.

chapter three

....

WIDE OPEN SPACES

F ast forward to starting high school, and all of the hormones that come with it. My incessant need to find my place in my class, school, and home life had started to become a huge priority and one that I struggled with on the daily.

Growing out of my elementary school bully phase and entering into the melodramatic and egocentric phase felt like cannonballing into a pool of freezing water. I jumped all in, only to find myself struggling to catch my breath after crashing into the ice-cold water. I found myself either flailing my arms reaching for the edge of the pool or waiting for someone's hand to help me out of that endless abyss.

At 14-years-old, life felt vastly different, as now mine was consumed with friends, keeping up with the current boyfriend statuses, and extracurricular activities. Actual schoolwork was a formality. My life rotated around matching scrunchies with Lauren and the comfiest sweatshirt I could find to hide my changing body shape. Mark was now a senior and would harass me at home if any word got back to him of what I was up to. My business was his business since it affected his coolness factor.

One day, I walked down the crowded senior hallway weaving past upperclassmen who, at the time, seemed perfect in every way. As the bell rang, I scanned the hall, amidst the closing lockers and swishing of hair, looking for his familiar red hair, I heard the comments and snickering start.

"Web, your *sister's* here," one voice tormented. Web was my brother's nickname, eventually being passed down from sibling to sibling.

"Hey, *Sister!*" said another, knowing full well that's what my brothers called me growing up instead of my actual name.

I approached Mark, and he and his massive, senior linebacker-looking friends seemed to tower over me as a lanky freshman. He closed his locker and turned around looking annoyed that I dared walk down his hallway and approach him.

"You're still giving me a ride home tonight, right?" I asked.

"Nah, I'm gonna run out to Miller's after practice. You'll have to figure it out," Mark responded nonchalantly, ignoring the grins and stares that were behind him facing me.

"But you know there's no late bus. How am I supposed to get home?" I pleaded; silently dying inside that he's purposely making this worse than it had to be.

"Web, I'll give her a ride home," a classmate teased.

Mark glared at him and then turned back to me. "Wait for me after practice. I'll come back and get you, but it will be a while. Otherwise, find a ride home with someone else," he said. Feeling that same disappointment and not being wanted I became so familiar with as a little sister, I watched Mark shut his locker, start back with the jeering comments with his buddies, and walk off to his next class.

In my hallway, I found the familiar faces of my friends sitting on the floor with their backs against the lockers and legs straight out in the hall, making it impossible for others to walk through.

Thick into a mix of discussion of music, homework and the latest CD coming out, I slid down my locker, finding a spot on the floor, and leaned my head on my boyfriend Nathan's shoulder, feeling defeated. As a varsity wrestler, his body was more filled out than the average lanky 16-year-old, and I loved how his shoulders rounded out and how my head felt on them.

"He may or may not come back and pick me up," I said. "Ugh, he always knows how to do that."

"What?" Nathan asked, grabbing my hand to put into his and feeling that magnetic pull he had over me. Even after a year of dating, his charismatic charm never ceased, and I was always drawn to him.

"Rub it raw. Everything's always a joke to him. Even me," I replied.

"I'll take you home," he offered. "I'll ask Bruce, but I'm sure it'll be fine. It's Bruce. He loves you. Besides, we always go through Beltrami on our way, anyway."

Feeling a glimmer of hope, I lifted my head and turned to look at him in his ice blue eyes I loved. Soaking in his handsome dark hair, pointed nose, and wide smile, I felt a sense of relief. Bruce was Nathan's dad and a beloved staple of our school. He was not only a paraprofessional, but the favored bus driver for sports and pseudo-assistant coach for football, wrestling, and track. He was a fixed feature on the sidelines, always motivating the team and quick to show the lesson after a loss. Bruce was as big as a grizzly bear, and at times looked like it with his grizzly beard and unkempt hair but was more of a teddy bear when it came to helping others. Underdogs were his favorite, as he saw potential in everybody.

I replied, "Really?! You mean that?"

"Absolutely, Gorgeous," he reassured me. "Anything for you."

31

I scrambled to get up and started down the hall before the bell, which was imminent. "I'll run and tell my mom really quick!" Smiling from ear to ear, feeling light on my toes with a flutter in my soul, I craved feeling this more, especially with him. Nathan was everything I thought I needed. The rest of life was just semantics.

I was in *love*.

Not just puppy love that many teenagers experience, but a genuine, magnetic, intertwined hearts kind of love. Our connection was intense and deep as if our souls collided. I was sure some sort of karmic explosion happened that would link us together forever.

•••

I have always been confident and assertive. I have never been afraid to put myself out there to see what would happen. As an instigator, I pushed boundaries and edges than what was considered normal. And "traditional" was lost on me, even though I dreamed of fairytales and happy endings where the boy chases after the girl, I wasn't willing to wait around. I went after what I wanted. And I wanted Nathan.

It's no surprise I asked him to be my boyfriend. I'm a get-to-the-point kinda girl, so in true eighth grade literary fashion, I wrote a note featuring one question with two options. *"Will you be my boyfriend? Yes or No."* We had just gotten back from Christmas break, where I spent the entire time agonizing on the phone with Lauren if I should or shouldn't ask him. With a made-up mind, I left the note in his locker during lunch and held my breath and felt nauseous for the next two hours until I received a response after seventh period. In his scraggly handwriting, I had a ripped out, half sheet of notebook paper with the answer I wanted. *"Yes."*

Once official, we jumped in deep. Our relationship became

32

magnetic. Meaning, we could be inseparable, and our energies would flow and intertwine together that it was hard to see where he ended, and I began. We would finish each other's sentences. Yet, it didn't take much for us to be in contrast; we were opposites pushing against each other.

However, just as with any teenage love, drama was sure to follow. Nathan had a severe case of jealousy, and I craved the attention, so I tiptoed the line with flirting regularly. Not only did I try to get attention from other boys, but Nathan also upped his attention game, and I adored every second of it. Now that I was finally the center of someone's world, I basked in it. Together, we made sense. He a wrestler; me a wrestling cheerleader. He smart and athletic, me musical, funny. He an introvert; me an extrovert. A complete mix of yin and yang. Voted as cutest couple in our yearbook, we looked the part. And yet it was the internal connection that made us, us. Even at fifteen and sixteen years old, others could witness the joined spirit we had. We often found ourselves the center of many fights between other couples, wishing they had what we had.

After a year of dating and as thick as thieves, we were inseparable. As we sat in his small bedroom, I couldn't help but laugh watching Nathan interact with his two sisters, Jennifer and Carly, while dominating the video game remote. While playing *Doom*, he would dutifully explain how the game worked to win. Me, not caring about video games or even how to play, was more engrossed in being a member of Nathan's family.

"Take that!" he exclaimed, hitting the buttons on the remote harder as if it would make a bit of difference in killing her character faster.

"Nate, knock it off!" Jennifer replied. "Let me get past this level!"

He just laughed his hearty laugh, which made his eyes light up even more. Highly competitive, he wanted to win and took no mercy on anyone.

The Browns were your typical hard-working family living in rural America. Our families were very similar in that way. We didn't necessarily ever go without, but there was never a massive abundance of cash overflow to have all the bells and whistles. Hand-me-downs were very real and totally normal and accepted. They spent summer days outside, imaginations were encouraged, and family meals revolved around the extended daylight that seemed endless in northern Minnesota. Nathan was your quintessential middle child, sandwiched between two sisters.

As a very open and giving family, nothing was off limits. It was expected to give of yourself and ultimately, get along. Unlike my family, the Browns were very close, with no topics off limits, which I loved. They spoke freely about the hard stuff: sex, addictions, relationships, politics, and religion. Nathan was always up for a good debate, however, it had to be fair and equal. As a natural harmonizer, he was not one to go after anyone who was looking for a fight, but instead have a deep and fair discussion to debate both sides. That being said, he was not one to back down and was quite sure of himself which came out in true teenager fashion. The only difference is that Nathan was an old soul and knew deep down that he was sure, and his confidence was endearing, versus over-the-top.

Bruce was a jack-of-all trades yet always involved with encouraging kids through various activities. His mother Laurie was a social worker for the county and the heart of the family. She was quiet and had a strong maternal spirit about her, and her hugs were healing. She was a second mama to me in a sense, as she was always open and willing to listen without judgment. I suppose for seeing so much with kids and broken families through the system, she saw the importance of being present and open to keep conversations flowing. Nathan was close with his sisters, Jennifer and Carly. Much like with me, Nathan was very protective of them. He saw the best in everyone yet wanted everyone around him to reach their highest potential, his sisters included. Nathan had a drive and determination like no one I've ever met, and he had high expectations for those around him because he saw others' potentials.

For never having sisters or even brothers close enough in age to want to play, this was beyond amazing that all of us could hang out together, as they were so close. His room was full of hand-me-down furniture, clothes were strewn about, textbooks spilling out of his backpack and medals adorned the walls. I sat on his bed next to him, observing how he interacted with the game and simultaneously trash talked his sister whom he was playing against.

"Nope, you're done for," he joked. "Besides, if you can't beat me on this level, there's no way you'll be able to make it through the next one!"

"Fine, I'm done then," said Jennifer throwing down her controller. "C'mon, Carly. Let's go down and make something to eat. I'm starving!"

As the girls walked out, Nathan turned to me. I was laying on my stomach with my head propped in my hands, so when I looked up at him, the glare of the light fixture was right next to his head which made me squint.

"You want to eat?" he asked casually.

"Nah, I'm good," I replied, not ready to get up.

"Should we start our homework?" he asked.

"How about you just *do* my homework?" I offered instead. Not being great at Algebra, I needed all the help I could get. Thankfully, Nathan was a cute tutor and knew how to explain it in the basic layman's terms that I needed. And he rewarded with a kiss, so I didn't complain too much.

Nathan strived to prove his worthiness in the different areas of life. In sports, he was highly competitive and always cheered on those who put in heart and effort. In school, he wanted to be a Triple A scholar, meaning the student excelled in Academics, Arts, and Athletics, so grades were a high priority for him. Nathan felt he had a disadvantage in life because he didn't have a wealthy last name or came from a family of high degreed professionals, but he was going to change that. Engineering and law were his favored degrees that he was striving for; one where he could build and one where he could argue, his two favorite things.

"C'mon," he said as he grabbed his backpack and started pulling out his books on his bed. "Let's just get it over with so we can do something else."

. . .

After about twenty minutes, my eyes started glazing over the problems, as I didn't understand why letters had to be in math equations, so I rolled over onto my back and stared at his ceiling covered in fake glow-in-the-dark stars I had applied myself.

"What's your biggest fear?" I asked.

As a way to escape reality, Nathan and I often found ourselves immersed in philosophical discussions quite often. Plus, he was one who I could go deep with without worrying about what he thought of me, as he saw my true spirit. He got me like no one who I had ever met had gotten me before.

"Losing you," Nathan replied as he put his pencil down, knowing full well we wouldn't be getting back to our homework anytime soon.

"Why, though?" I pressed further. I didn't get it.

He lay down on his back next to me and stared at the same stars on his popcorn ceiling and sighed. "I don't know, but I do know that you're the most important thing in my entire world," he started to explain. "But it's more than that. It's like I would be broken if something ever happened to you, I couldn't live with myself."

He paused as I remained silent. It felt logical I thought, and yet inexplicable. As a 15-year-old, I never that anyone would ever feel that strongly about *me*.

Nathan continued, "I mean, I would hate to ever see you with another guy. I would want to punch him in the face or break a wall or key his car...but as long as I knew you were safe and happy, I'd be okay. But if you weren't here? I just can't..." he trailed off, and we lay silent for a bit longer. "What about you?" he asked.

"Me?" I replied, pausing for a few moments to think. "I think dying is scary. Like, I believe in Heaven and know it would be where I'd want to be, but actually dying? I don't like thinking like that. That freaks me out."

"Yeah..." We remained silent in our thoughts.

"What do you think Heaven is like?" I asked further. It was just this past year that Nathan started coming to church, with my family, no less. Knowing and seeing how important my faith was to me, he wanted to find a connection with God like I had.

After a moment, "Pretty. White. A lot of singing," Nathan responded. "I don't know...maybe you have supper with all of the angels, and you get to ask questions about your life and then joke about everything."

"I think Heaven has streets made with gold, almost like in the *Wizard of Oz*. And that my grandpa will be there when I arrive," I said, referencing the only person I knew who had died. "I sure hope there is a lot of laughing."

Sensing that Nathan was smiling, I turned my head to look at him. He turned his head towards mine, met my gaze and kissed my forehead. "See? Not scary! You don't have to be afraid." Continuing, he said, "Besides, I will never let anything happen to you. I would fight like hell to make sure you will always be safe." With a wink, he added, "You know me, I will knock out an angel or two if they were taking you away." His ice blue eyes contrasted his fiercely stubborn spirit.

"You'd do that for Duck or Garth, too," I retorted.

"Hell yeah, I would! They're my best friends! I'd do it for a bunch of people!" he shot back. "I'd stick my neck out for anyone who has been good to me."

Just then Nathan's dog, Bear, came sauntering in through the door and placed his wet, slobbery face next to mine looking for some attention. Laughing, I rolled over to greet him and love him up with some head scratches.

• • •

By the time tenth grade rolled around, I was seriously considering where I belonged. My relationship with Nathan was strong, and yet draining at the same time. I loved the idea of being in a relationship, yet it felt like so much work. I mean, I was 15. Shouldn't I be having fun and enjoying time with my friends and boyfriend versus always being emotionally invested in the relationship? Talking it over with my friends, no one else had it like this. It always felt heavy, and I was tired of being so energetically drained.

If I wasn't defending myself and how I felt to Nathan, I was busy holding him up emotionally. Nathan was diagnosed with depression at this time and started on new medication. Although I was happy that he was getting help and finding out answers to his highs and lows, I was scared and unsure what that all meant.

"Dammit, Gorgeous!" Nathan muttered as he slammed his

locker shut. "Why do you do this to me?"

"What?" I replied indignantly, not holding back. "What am I doing?" It was lunch hour, and senior high students scattered through the halls, milling about and waiting for the bell. Nathan's locker was down the hall from the music and band rooms and across from the wrestling room, near the gym where most students convened after lunch. Surely everyone was about to hear what was about to be discussed.

Nathan pulled me closer to him by his locker and looked intently into my eyes. He lowered his voice, and I could see him holding back his rage, "Not here."

"I'm not *doing* anything, Nate," I said in a louder than normal tone, pulling my arm out of his grip. "I was just talking to them. We are working on a project together. It has nothing to do with you! None of this ever has anything to do with you." He sulked and slammed his hand against the locker, making it reverberate and echo down the hall. So much that it scared a freshman girl just turning the corner.

"If you can't handle that I talk to other guys--friends--in our class, then you need to check yourself," I said. "You can't tell me who I can or cannot be friends with! Especially when these are guys I've grown up since Kindergarten!"

"Yeah, well I don't like them," Nate replied sulkily, his eyes lowered again. "I know guys. I know what how they talk, and I know what they want. And it's not going to be you."

"Get off it," I said, shaking my head. "You are ridiculous, and I won't have anything to do with this." I turned and furiously walked off to find Lauren in the gym and debrief, just to make sure I wasn't the crazy one.

The seventh period came around, and when I went to my locker,

I found a note from Nathan on the top shelf. *Always with the apology notes*, I thought. I grabbed it and walked off to my study hall. Still furious, I read it in the library, sitting next to the same guys that made Nate so jealous.

> *They don't get you like I do, Gorgeous*, it read. *I'm sorry I made you hate me like that. I'm just so pissed that they seem to have everything already. I'm trying. I'm battling these demons that tell me that I'm not worthy of you. I desperately want to give you the world, and I can't. I just don't want you to leave and find someone who can. I love you. Please don't hate me. I love you. -Nate*

I folded the letter back up and tried to ignore it while laughing and joking with everyone else, but my heart wasn't there. It was with Nathan and how heartsick I felt that he felt so broken inside. My thoughts instantly went to fixing mode. *How can I help him? How can I make him see how amazing he truly is and all that he has to offer?* Then they turned to more serious thoughts. *Is he taking his meds? Is this what depression is like? A roller coaster?*

Depression was a foreign concept to me and trying to regulate his emotional wellbeing felt like I was always walking on broken glass. I knew he was struggling, to which I unconsciously tried to fix by giving more of myself to him versus letting him navigate it on his own. I was screwing the both of us over. Those thoughts ran through my mind for the rest of the school day and into cheerleading practice. I was hitching a ride home with Nate, so I had to talk through this with him.

Leaning against the trophy case in the gym lobby, I waited after practice for Nate to get out of the locker room. I replayed all the scornful things I was going to tell him, so he could see my way, not his. I truly wanted to hurt him like he hurt me for trying to control our relationship. Other wrestlers were coming out, and soon I saw him turn the corner.

He smiled his million-dollar white smile.

"Gorgeous," he breathed to himself. "You're a sight for sore eyes."

Instantly, I melted. I always did. The fire that raged inside earlier were now embers. Still burning, but not to the extent that once was. I was able to forget the deep-rooted issue in our relationship for the time being.

"I'm sorry," he whispered as he leaned into my ear. My eyes closed, I smiled as I inhaled his cologne.

As he pulled away to look me in the eyes, I tried my best to stand my ground to honor my stubborn spirit. "You can't be like that," I said.

"I know, I'm working on it," he replied. He took my hand into his and said, "You know you're the most important thing in my life. I just don't want to lose you."

"You won't," I reassured him, squeezing his hand. "But we need to work on those demons you keep talking about."

Nate got real serious real fast. "I know," he confessed. "I'm working on it. My meds help, but I think I need more."

Just then, Bruce and Jennifer came into the lobby to meet us. "Ready to roll?" Bruce asked. Nate nodded and grabbed my bag along with his as we walked out to the car, an old, two-tone blue Chevy Citation. We crawled into the backseat while Bruce and Jennifer were in the front.

"How can I help you?" I whispered, while Bruce and Jennifer recapped their day in the front seat.

"I don't know," Nate said defeated. "Maybe I need a shrink to figure out my head. You know I have all these thoughts and fears and shit. I can't make sense of any of them. I'm trying at school. I'm trying to get teachers to like me. I'm trying to do music. I'm trying to keep weight. I'm trying to keep you happy. And then I see you with someone else and I just lose it. I can't seem to get control over anything anymore."

"So, you try with me," I offered softly. "I mean...I get it, but I certainly don't like it."

"I know," he said.

I looked out past Nathan, through the window into the dark, wintery sky. "I wish you could see you the way I see you." I wanted to fix Nathan. Not that he was broken, but that I felt and saw his potential and knew with someone to believe in him, he could soar. I witnessed the light he had in his soul and saw how desperately he wanted others to see it, too, so I cracked him open to keep going; to keep showing up so that they would.

"Funny," Nate replied. "That's what I pray every night for you, too."

• • •

By Spring of 2000, Nathan and I were both quite fried, emotionally. The back and forth of jealousy, anger, and control on top of teenage hormones had taken its toll on our relationship. The thought of taking a break from each other was terrifying yet sounded like sweet relief. We were in a constant state of turmoil, rolling on waves of highs and then crashing into deep lows. Unable to navigate the waters, we became tumultuous towards each other. Together, yet distant. Nathan and I often thought we would be better off separate, yet we were both scared at actually taking that next step. I sought reprieve in my friends and dreamed of what it would be like to date or kiss another boy. I looked around at the guys in my class and school, and although it felt invigorating to think about, I knew these guys their whole life and couldn't imagine a relationship with them. It would be just a kiss or a date just for the sake of having fun... nothing serious.

But there *was* someone who I enjoyed flirting with. Someone who seemed exotic and yet innocent since nothing was there. A boy in my confirmation class, who went to a different school. Someone that Nathan barely knew and flirting that I could get away with since Nathan wasn't in our confirmation class and I didn't have to explain myself. My flirting, however, was not anything to be desired. The loudmouth that I was, I resorted to teasing and picking on this shy, quiet boy. However, he didn't seem to mind and played along with me. It seemed innocent enough because we only saw each other for a couple hours each week, and he knew I had a boyfriend, so in my eyes, nothing could happen. And yet, deep down, I knew a spark was there between us. And I really, really liked it.

In between the highs and lows of Nathan, I was still searching to find myself in my class and school. My body was growing, my legs were longer, and I was working on my coordination to excel in volleyball; just in time for Junior Olympics tryouts. Around this time, I started to rock at vocal solos and ensembles. The only thing that was holding me back was what others would think of me. I doubted myself and downplayed my talent, as I didn't want to come across as cocky, and surely there were others that were better than I was. As the funny, musical girl in a very cliquey class, I was far from popular. I was ambiguous, being able to adapt and get along with the various cliques. I felt like such an outsider, always looking in. It was a theme that would follow me from home to school and through the later years in life; trying to find my place among the crowd.

My relationship with my mom was quite strained, as well. My teenage angst came out in a mega attitude that didn't fare so well with her. Since I have always been an early riser, I loved going to school with my mom before the bus. I loved the quietness of the school before 8 a.m. It was like the calm before the storm. Plus, not having to endure the cold bus rides was a perk.

"What else is on the agenda today, Babe?" my mom asked with affection as we drove in the car. We were halfway to Fertile, and I was sitting cross-legged in the front seat staring out the window.

"Practice," I replied, uninspired to talk at 7:15 a.m.

"Did you finish your project for Geometry?" she asked, knowing full well that I procrastinated doing any sort of math until the very last minute.

"Nope."

"Will you be going to Lauren's after school before practice?"

"Probably," I said, still staring out the window, not engaging in the conversation.

After a long pause, my mom cracked. "Every morning. We do this every single morning! You know, you don't have to drive with me. There is a bus that drives right by the house that you can get on. Maybe you should think about riding it until your attitude changes, and you're able to have a conversation without it." Taken aback, I turned to her with wide eyes. "I'm serious, Kathryn," she went on. "This is my time of peace before a long, chaotic day, and I don't need to have it start it out like this. Starting tomorrow, you will ride the bus. You let me know when you're ready to ride with me again."

I sat silently wondering what just happened. *That came out of left field*, I thought. *Doesn't she understand? Can't she see what I'm going through? Doesn't she know how fried I am?* There was nothing left to give; I was in survival mode. We rode the remaining several miles in silence. On the verge of tears, I recounted what just happened. *Great. Now even my mom doesn't want me around*, I thought.

I remembered 10-year-old me with the green glasses and permed bob in fourth grade. My mom loved hosting her teacher friends to a holiday party every December, and the detail and finishes that she put into the beautiful reception were astounding: fine apple cider with cinnamon sticks simmering, our Christmas tree trimmed with elegance and sophistication, the plethora of fresh baked goodies and treats for all to enjoy, and the buzz of gathering which my mom loved the most. I loved it, too, as it felt like for a brief moment in time, all the attention was on us.

But what I distinctly remembered driving to school that day, was the same feeling that I had as a 10-year-old at my mom's holiday party. Before the first guest arrived, a thorough inspection of the house was done, and everything was up to par except for one room: My room. Nonchalantly, my mother stopped at my door and sighed. "Still, Kathryn? You couldn't clean your room?" she said. She proceeded to close my door shut. "We will be placing jackets on the bed in my room instead." I stood there not understanding what I did wrong. *So, what if my room is messy? It's my room.* My heart took that comment and action personally. My room didn't fit in with her seemingly perfect life. I felt like I didn't fit in with her seemingly perfect life.

I guess nothing's changed. I still don't fit in her seemingly perfect life, I thought as I stared out the window as we drove into town.

• • •

The first weekend in March, Nathan and I had just come back from the Minnesota State Wrestling tournament with his family. It was around that time that everyone else could sense how unsteady our relationship had become as even Nathan's sisters asked about it while us girls were holed up in our own hotel room during the previous nights.

"What's up with you and Nate?" Jennifer asked as she sat down on the bed while I was digging into my bag for my curling iron. Carly stood quietly in the bathroom pretending to ignore what Jennifer had just said.

45

"What?" I asked, pretending to be shocked.

"Oh, come on," she exaggerated, throwing herself back on the bed. "You two are like hissing cats to one another! Besides," she sat back up, "he already told us everything. I want to hear it from you." They wanted my version of what was going on because they had already heard Nate's, complete with moping around the house and writing letters to me just to throw them away.

"If you already know, then there's no use of me repeating it," I said huffily. Already pissed that this was how we were starting off the weekend, I made sure Nate knew exactly how annoying I could be the for remaining time we were there. Not ready to completely break it off and yet, not completely together, Nathan and I were in limbo. He was still my best friend and the person who knew me inside and out. When I needed to talk or to ask for help, technically he was still my go-to, because even Lauren didn't get me the way Nate did. That's probably why we strung each other along for so long. We loved each other and knew we had a deeper connection than we could ever explain, so to give that up cold turkey in the midst of high school drama where we would see each other every day was a hard decision.

And yet, there were rumblings of drama that I couldn't entirely ignore. Rumors of misgivings that seemed so far-fetched as rumors most often are, and yet somewhere in the back of my mind, I questioned if they were true. Being a feisty one that cuts to the chase, I hot-headedly walked in and confronted him, just a short two weeks later.

"Are they true?"

"What?" Nathan jumped as I blindsided him in the weight room.

"The rumors," I impatiently explained. "Are they true?" Knowing full well he knew what I was talking about, I was not going to get into the details for his satisfaction. Rumors had been spreading that Nathan was making rounds with a classmate of ours; getting caught in the tunnel, meeting in the weight room, being seen together outside by his car. All of these were seemingly innocent, except for the fact that it was her spreading the rumors. It seemed laughable as they were an odd combination; she was not his type and she had a history of getting around. Plus, the thought of Nathan cheating was beyond me.

Dropping his weights, he walks towards me. "No! Absolutely not!" Nathan exclaimed. "She is lying. I would never do that to you! I could never do that to you. And with her? No. Just, no."

I stared intently into his eyes. The rage boiled within me at the thought of her spreading blatant lies. Nathan pulled me closer and I could feel the swell of his upper body workout and the sweat beading. I looked down at my shoes to keep the tears from welling any more. *Of course he wouldn't cheat on me!* I thought to myself. *Especially with her? We're like the perfect couple... and she? Well, she is not even on the radar.* I talked myself down for the time being.

"Okay," I receded, pulling away from him. My blue green eyes met his as I held out my right pinky and asked, "Pinky promise?" To us, that symbolized a soul promise, never to be broken. He had only done it once before early on in our relationship and saw how heartbroken I was, so he vowed never to break a pinky promise again.

"Pinky promise," he said lovingly as he pulled me back in to hold me close.

And that's all I needed; all I ever needed. Even though I could be so enraged, I still trusted him with my heart and soul.

47

*"Storms make trees
take deeper roots."*

- Dolly Parton

chapter four

....

WEATHERING THE STORM

I t was a typical Sunday. My family got up bright and early for 8:30 am Mass, with Sunday dinner to follow. Nathan and I had plans to finish a dreaded geometry project, so he showed up around 1:00 pm. I think Nathan secretly wanted to save our relationship by spending more time together, but I was just happy to get out of the house and to have help with my homework.

"Want to drive to my house?" he asked. It was March 26th, a few months before I turned Sweet Sixteen, so I only had my driver's permit.

His house was 17 miles south of Beltrami and a road I'd driven a thousand miles before; straight with an S curve marking halfway. In the prairie where we lived, most roads were sectioned off in square miles, with farms strategically placed along marking their land.

"Sure," I replied, and he handed me his keys.

"Do you want to do the jump?" he asked as we drove, referring to the deep washout that was created every spring when the snow thawed. It was right by a big culvert which made for excellent air when launching a little car like a Citation.

"Absolutely!" I responded.

"Good. Turn here," he said, pointing at the next gravel road to

49

the right. I made my way down the road, accelerating as we neared the approach. Gravel roads still gave me the heebie-jeebies, so I was cautious not to get too fast but gunned it as we cleared the jump. That old Citation made some air and hit the ground like a ton of bricks as we continued on, laughing together.

Knowing that we missed the left turn by the culvert, so we could jump it, I drove down to the next turn an extra mile out of the way.

• • •

When I awoke, I was confused as to what just happened. I stood up from the cold, hard ground and looked around, trying to process why I was in the field and what time of day it was. There were no leaves on the trees, and the blackened dirt still had the tracks from last fall's harvest. As I flipped my jacket off that was covering my head, I turned to my left to see the old Chevy Citation sitting on all four tires in the field, too.

Still not fully grasping what was happening, yet noticing it was a brisk March day, I tried to bend down and grab my jacket to put back on.

Only I couldn't. I felt an instant pain and stopped.

Where am I? Why am I in the field? Disorientated, not recognizing anything, I started walking towards the car, roughly 500 yards away. It felt like I was walking in slow motion, hearing every crunch of the step puncture an eerie silence around me. As I got closer, I saw his body and cried out in terror.

Nathan's two legs stuck out from underneath the car and I instantly remembered. We were driving to his house. I tried to jump the culvert. I couldn't bend down and check on him, so I told him that I would get help.

"Don't move! I will save you! Please, God! Keep him safe because I need him!"

The car sat as if nothing had happened to it, like someone had drove it out on the frozen field and parked it. The windshield was blown out, yet all four tires were still intact, and there was hardly any damage to the exterior from the multiple flips that incurred.

I saw a farm about a quarter of a mile away.

As a farm girl, I knew that cutting across fields and farms is the fastest way to get to anywhere worth going, so that's what I did. My Chuck Taylors were not holding up too well with the semi-frozen ground, and my feet began to get wet and cold. Crunching through the unthawing weeds and grass in the ditch, I didn't even notice the standing water and mud from the spring rain the day earlier until I felt the suction of the mud as I tried to lift my foot. It gripped left shoe and pulled it off my foot. I didn't dare bend down to retrieve it, so I kept stumbling along.

Once back on the road, I finally stopped and looked down at myself. One shoe, jeans with mud at the hem, my favorite black sweater with a cream stripe down the arms, and a newly dislocated wrist. Dislocated to the point of seeing my thumb where my pinkie was supposed to be. Knowing that wasn't right, I used my right hand to hold it together where it was supposed to be to keep the blood circulating, tight against my chest. I didn't want to look at it again, so I kept walking.

The farm seemed like an eternity away, but I was determined to get help. *He needs it.* Through their ditch, tree row, and grass, I walked straight up to the yellow house. I still don't know what time it was or how long it had been since we were in the car driving, but I knew time was of the essence. I let my left wrist fall limp as I let go of it to knock with my right hand. Feverishly, I knocked. No one was answering.

I knocked again, harder.

A boy not much older than me answered in a black t-shirt and jeans.

"Please, I need help!" I insisted. "Nathan. He needs help. Our car crashed in that field. Please, call 911!"

His eyes opened wide as I rambled on and the look on his face was horrified. "Yes, I'll call 911," he replied. "I know Nathan. I'll call the Browns." We were less than two miles from Nate's house. The boy rushed out of sight while I stood outside waiting.

I saw the familiar blue Chevy Citation fly down the road, picking up as much dust from the gravel as possible. Bruce, Nathan's dad. I saw him stop at the accident and get out, then the car continued on to the farm where I was. Laurie, Nate's mom got out and tried to give me the biggest hug I could have ever imagined, but I winced in pain. She placed her arms around me and embraced me for the longest time, as if she already knew.

"The ambulance is on the way," she said. "Can you get in the car?"

"My back hurts," I stuttered.

"We will wait, then." She placed her arm back around my shoulders and held me close. I didn't realize I was shivering until I felt her warmth. Standing in the driveway of someone else's farmstead, waiting for the ambulance and not talking made everything feel so much bigger and longer. We stood in silence, looking down the gravel road past the tree lines to see the car still sitting in the field. It was as if we were in the eye of the storm.

Both of us prayed.

And then, we all heard it.

The wail of the siren exploded in the cool, afternoon air like a bullhorn. The ambulance didn't come into sight right away, but when it's rural Minnesota in the spring, sound travels for miles. When it came into sight, we watched it first stop at the scene of the accident. Good, I thought. *He needs help.* Moments later, the second ambulance came. This one was for me. It stopped at the scene and then proceeded to come down the gravel road and turn at the farmstead to where I was. As it approached, it had cut the siren but kept the lights flashing.

The paramedics were surprised to see me standing there. Clearly by the sight of me, they could tell time was a factor. "Can you tell me what happened?" they asked.

"The car hit the ditch and when I woke up, I walked here for help," I offered, standing with my wrist to my chest and in shock as to what all was happening. They asked if anything hurt and I bravely and cautiously showed my hand. I also noted that my back hurt when I tried to bend over to get my jacket when I first woke up, so they got out the gurney and were about to load me into the ambulance.

As I laid on the hard gurney, I heard the thunderous sound overhead before I saw it. Like a scene out of a *James Bond* movie, I see a chopper descending and gracefully land on the same gravel road that we just careened off of. As they shut the doors of the ambulance, I could still hear the deafening whooshing of the rotating propellers from a quarter mile away.

Not fully comprehending the severity of the accident or our injuries, I was confused why the ambulance stopped by the chopper. Maybe we have to wait for it to take off with him before we can go, I thought. But the back doors opened, and the paramedics started taking my gurney out.

"Kathryn, you parents have just arrived. They will follow the helicopter to Fargo and will be waiting for you there," the paramedic explained.

"This is for me?" I asked. "I don't understand."

"Yes, you will be airlifted to MeritCare in Fargo," he said.

Still not comprehending what was happening, I asked, "Can I see my dad?"

Why I asked for my dad, I still don't know. We were never real close growing up and with always chasing after my two older brothers, I felt that I was always forgotten; the little sister always left behind. And yet at this very moment I needed him. When I saw his face come into focus as I laid in the back of the helicopter, I started to cry. The first tears that I shed since the adrenaline was wearing off and reality was hitting me. *I am being life-flighted to the hospital.*

"Dad?" I sobbed as I reached out to grab his hand. "I'm sorry. I'm so sorry."

"Kathryn! Everything is going to be okay," my dad yelled over the propellers as he grabbed my arm. "Your mom and I will follow you to Fargo. Everything is going to be okay."

The paramedics said they were ready and it was time to go. Hearing all the system checks and looking around at the impressive gauges and medical equipment, it was overwhelming to fully understand everything that was going on. I asked the paramedic, "What's your name?"

"Darren," he replied.

"Darren, I'm scared," I confessed.

"I know, Kathryn. We will be at the hospital in less than half an hour. You are safe, and we will get you some answers after they can run some tests," Darren explained.

"Okay," I replied, trying hard as I could to hold back the tears that were brimming. Now I was petrified. My mind was swirling with questions. After a few moments I asked, "Will you hold my hand?" Darren reached over to hold my hand and sat with me in silence until we had arrived just a short and impressive 23 minutes later. By car, the drive to Fargo was well over an hour, so it felt like nothing and we were already landing.

● ● ●

The next few hours seem like a blur. Once in the emergency room, as soon as I was moved from the gurney to a bed, the action started. The female doctor awaiting my arrival greeted me by name and offered hers. She then explained what was going to happen next: CAT scans, x-rays, and blood tests.

"When will I get to see my mom?" asking the most important question.

"When you are all done," she replied as she was assessing monitors. She then stopped and looked me in the eyes realizing I was a terrified 15-year-old girl and gently said, "Soon."

They took out the fabric scissors and started to cut off my clothes. "But these are my favorite jeans and sweater! And I'm wearing a brand-new Victoria's Secret bra! Please, let me take them off. I promise I won't sue you!"

"Kathryn, we have to. We don't know what your injuries are, and we have to get you ready for x-rays," the female doctor explained. I silently sobbed as I heard the unabashedly cutting of my favorite clothes, pulling out my ponytail, removing my rings and earrings, and finally taking out my contacts. They were stripping me of anything I thought that made me, me, when all they were truly doing was stripping me down to the real me. "We need to fix your wrist. It's turning blue and we can't wait much longer," the doctor explained. "This is going to hurt. Are you ready?"

Taking a deep breath, I held it and muffled a scream as she pulled my dislocated wrist out and back onto where it belongs to reset it. Instantaneous, blood started circulating again and the color started to come back.

"Wow! You took that like a champ!" she exclaimed. "Not even a shot of whiskey or a bullet in the teeth to bear down on!" I glared at her for thinking that was even remotely funny or impressive.

Not long after, I was whisked away for an x-ray. After multiple CAT Scans, an MRI, and numerous pokes and prods later, I was back in the ER triage room, waiting to see my mom. The curtain pulled back and I finally saw my mom come in, her eyes red from her tears she wiped away right before she walked in. She came in alone, my dad still in the lobby. And yet, she was the best sight I could have ever seen at that moment; my entire heart was in front of me. What I didn't know or fully understand what she was holding onto and what she was about to say.

After her staring at me, fully assessing that I was, in fact, okay, she opened up. "Babe, I have to tell you something," she affectionately said with tears surfacing and holding my hand. "I'm sorry, Babe, but Nathan didn't make it. He's gone." A quiet sob broke from her as she tried so hard to remain strong.

Confused and still disoriented of the day and what all transpired, I questioned, "What do you mean he didn't make it?"

It was as if I was having a total out of body experience up to that moment, and when she said those words, I collided right back down into my body and felt everything. Physical and emotional heartbreak, mental anguish, and utter shock.

In nothing more than a whisper, she said, "They say he didn't feel a thing, but his heart was still beating by the time they got him to the hospital. They tried to save him, but there was too much internal damage." She searched my eyes. "Babe, they just couldn't do anything more."

His heart was still beating. He was alive, and they couldn't save him? This can't be happening. He was supposed to help me with my Geometry homework. We aren't supposed to be here. This isn't happening. This isn't real. How could everything I have known for the past two years, everything I've felt for someone be gone? Just like that? I squeezed my eyes shut trying not to see, not to think, not to feel. *This isn't happening. This isn't real. I am not alone. God wouldn't do this to me,* I kept repeating over and over in my head.

Jolting me out of my thoughts, my mom continued. "Babe, a police officer is here, and he needs to talk to you. Your dad and I will be right outside, but he needs to hear what happened from you," she explained. "Alone."

"Okay," still numb with questions and thoughts. She left, and a tall Minnesota State Trooper came in behind the curtain. He took off his brown Mountie hat and held it under his arm as he pulled out a notepad and pen. He introduced himself to me and in a matter-of-fact voice, said he needed to hear what happened in detail.

After a few questions, I explained that after lunch around 1:30 pm, Nathan picked me up in Beltrami. As farm kids, we all knew how to drive, and since I had my permit and it was a little over a month to my 16th birthday, I wanted to drive. I explained how we took the gravel road a mile north of his house because it had the big dip from the culverts that was fun to drive on and how I missed the turn to head south, so instead of slamming on the breaks, we went to the next section mile. Once we got to Nathan's road, we were two miles away, driving east.

"Do you remember how fast you were going?" the state trooper asked.

"No. Maybe 45-50?" guessing as I never looked down at the speedometer.

"And where were you headed?"

"To Nathan's house to do my geometry homework," I replied.

"Were you wearing seatbelts?" he asked, knowing full well the answer to that question.

"No. They were cut out of the car," I said.

"Do you remember what happened before the crash?" he pressed on. "Were you distracted? Were you talking? Did you veer to one side or the other?"

"The road was spongy," I replied, almost on autopilot at this point. "Like when it has fresh gravel, but it wasn't." Trying to explain the softened road, wet from the spring and rain the day before. Thinking back to hours earlier, I remembered the way Nathan's hand felt in mine as I reached out and turned to look at him with a sweet smile and heavy heart; somehow knowing we weren't going to be together forever like my 15-year-old heart originally wanted. Our relationship was hanging on by a thread and we both knew it. Nathan looked at me with a smile and said, *"I love you."* The last words I would hear from him. Ever.

"I had one hand on the wheel and I was looking at Nathan," I said. "We hit a mushy spot on the road and the car started to veer to the left so Nathan grabbed the steering wheel to try to correct it, only he pulled too hard," explaining the facts with my one non-casted hand, knowing full well the Trooper didn't want to hear about some 15-year-old's puppy love. "When he let go, I overcorrected back to the left and we hit the ditch." Shutting my eyes, I flashed back to the thud of the impact in the ditch and seeing the blue sky as we launched into the air before the second impact and subsequent rolls of the car as we ejected from the car.

"Do you remember anything else?" he asked.

"No," I replied, done with reliving it, never wanting to go back there again. At this point, I was fully numb. I didn't feel as if I was truly there, but for the second time that day, witnessing this exchange from above my body. When we were done, the state trooper said goodbye and both of my parents came in. I was able to ask more questions and start to piece together not only the events of that day, but the remnants that were left of my life. The doctor on-call opened up the curtain to my small area of the emergency room and pulled up a small, black stool to my bedside.

It was then that I learned the extent of my injuries.

BROKEN

"You are lucky to be alive, young lady," Dr. Trainor said as he adjusted the stool and gently put his hand on my casted wrist. "You know full well that you fractured and dislocated wrist, but you also fractured three vertebrae in your lower back. Vertebrae L1, L2, and L3, which is why your back hurt when you tried to grab your jacket. They were clean breaks, meaning straight through, but if you would've bent down to get your jacket, those vertebrae would have shifted, which would have punctured your spinal cord and more than likely you would've been paralyzed."

Paralyzed? I thought. *What is he talking about? I'm not paralyzed; I walked for help. I'm fine. Why couldn't they save Nathan?*

He kept going. "You also fractured both ankles and have three bruised ribs. One of those ribs punctured your right lung, which is why it hurts to breathe. Lastly, the remnants of your broken vertebrae cut a big gash in your spleen, so you have some internal bleeding, which we are keeping a close eye on. It doesn't look like you need surgery right now, but it's not off the table." Dr. Trainor leaned in closer and looked me in the eyes, "It is a miracle that you are alive, young lady."

This is ridiculous.

"If I broke all of those bones, how did I walk for help?" I asked, perplexed as to how all of that could have happened to me.

"Adrenaline. You didn't feel much, did you?" Dr. Trainor asked.

"No, I guess not. I just knew I needed to get him help," finally realizing that my effort was fruitless. Nathan still didn't make it. Thoughts swirled in my head. *Why'd they whisk me away when he was the one who needed the help? I tried to save him, why couldn't they take him first?*

Others came in to the ER to see me, like my dad and brother, our priest, a few friends, but I was not even there. I was trying to pick up the pieces of what used to be my life and it now resembled more of a scattered puzzle with pieces missing, rather than anything I used to know.

According to my mom, the Emergency Room waiting room was full of friends and family who came to support me and my family. I was given the blessed sacrament of the Anointing of the Sick by our hometown priest, something usually reserved for those in critical condition. My best friend Lauren had made it, only after going to the Grand Forks hospital first, thinking I was there, just to drive the extra hour and fifteen minutes to Fargo. Again, thinking that life was just like the movies and because I have always wanted the happily ever after like in those said movies, where the lead character, "Doesn't want them to see me like this," I refused to see her. It's not that I didn't want to see her, but I thought that's just what you do. I didn't realize that most people came to support me and my family because of the severity of my injuries and wondering if I'd make it. I had no idea.

I convinced Nathan to be an organ donor when he got his license the year before, never thinking he would ever be a donor, yet just a short year later, someone special was getting his beautiful, ice blue eyes. Once I was out of the ER and situated, I found myself in the Intensive Care Unit. Again, not fully grasping how critical I actually was. As the night went on, I found myself in huge amounts of pain, as I ended up being physically ill from medications and needed to vomit. When ordered to lay flat on your back with zero movement, puking becomes a challenge, as aspirating on it was a very real scenario. Plus, not having a cast on my back meant that any movement could shift the vertebrae and pinch my spinal cord. Every time I got sick, I was strapped to a spinal board which they flipped me on my side, while my mom held my hair and the plastic mauve tray that my tears and vomit fell into.

I spent the next five days in the Pediatric ICU, where I was poked and prodded which seemed like every hour. I also was fitted for a turtle shell back brace, a dream come true for any teen girl. Having two male and one female orthotic specialists come in to measure you, naked, from collar bone to pelvis and rib to rib is absolutely mortifying. To feel their cold, sterile hands place a ribbon tape measure around your body for circumference all while trying not to cry is beyond comprehension. As if the trauma of the accident itself wasn't horrifying enough, add in the emotional trauma of strangers knowing and touching every inch of your body to document it.

As I lay there, silently sobbing, praying for it to be over, I memorized the walls and all of the equipment in the room. I was not going to look at these people. I squeezed my eyes shut and to this day, I still have the imprint of the sterile room and can see the classroom clock on the white wall above the sliding glass door out of my room. I then was moved to the Pediatrics floor. When asked why, they told me it was because I was 15 and still technically a kid. Plus, they wavered back and forth and this way I was ensured a private room, so my mom could stay and extra special care since they were a children's hospital.

I had plenty of visitors, and one of them being Bruce who came every day after school to see me. I truly think it was because he had to see for himself that I was okay, but also because I was his last link to Nathan. Sure, he had his family and Nathan's friends, but he and I both knew that Nate and I were inseparable and had a soul connection. So when Bruce saw me, he saw Nate, too.

I was never alone while in the hospital, as someone was always there with me. My mom was able to stay with me in my room each night other than when I was in the ICU, where she slept on the couch in the waiting room. My dad came every day after chores, and Mark graced his presence after class, both meeting just in time for supper.

"You got a lot of mail today," my dad said as he walked into my room and plopping the stack on my bed.

"Holy!" I exclaimed, grabbing my letter opener. The best part of my day was receiving mail, to which my nurses helped decorate on the wall of my room to add more cheer than the drab, institutionalized look the walls originally gave. Today's haul was a mix of cards and presents, one notably being a journal from my English teacher who knew how much I loved to write.

Just then, Mark breezed in with a wide smile on his face. "Hey-o!" he announced his arrival. Noticing the new wheelchair that graced its presence in my room, he took a seat in it and started wheeling around. "Ooohhhh, when did you get this?"

I put all the mail on my bedside tray table. "They brought it for me to go to see Nathan," I explained. Not knowing how to handle a heavy bomb like that, Mark shifted gears.

"Huh. Did you do any wheelies down the hall with it yet?" He smiled that wide smile and I laughed, knowing that would've been the first thing Mark would've done if he had a wheelchair. Just then my mom walked back in. She had just gotten back from daily mass at the cathedral across the street. Catching up on the events that she missed, along with reading all of the cards that I got, she was back up to speed.

"Where do you want to go tonight?" asked my mom, knowing

full well Mark had an idea already.

"Definitely not Grandma's Kitchen," he said. "We worked on their fry baskets today, and now I'm scarred for life." Mark was going to the Technical College for welding, where they worked on various projects ranging from tractors and trucks to designing art projects to commercial work for local restaurants and businesses. "How about TGI Friday's?"

Turning towards me, my mom asked, "Kathryn, will you be okay if we all go?"

"Will anybody be here with me?" I asked.

"I already asked Rhonda to check in on you in between her rounds," my mom reassured.

Just then Rhonda peeked in, hearing her name. "You got it, girl! It's slow tonight, so I can hang while your parents are gone." She smiled, waved, and as quick as she entered, she left to finish her rounds.

"Well, we better get going," my mom said as she stood. "Mark, are you riding with us?"

"Nah, I'll just meet you there," he replied.

Since I was in the hospital for two weeks, I missed Nathan's funeral. There was talk that I was going to be released on special orders just to attend the funeral and come straight back to the hospital, but since I was still so fragile, that didn't happen. And yet, because we're from such a close, small knit town, people tend to do move mountains to make miracles happen. Mine came in the form of a private prayer service with Nathan.

The local funeral home director brought Nathan down the day before the funeral. That is where I was finally able to see him and say goodbye; to have closure. It was only five days after the accident, and I couldn't even walk yet, so I was in a wheelchair trying to reconnect with my best friend. Nothing was real about it. I wasn't myself and Nate wasn't himself. We were two souls in strange bodies that didn't recognize each other, which was hard to comprehend. I am grateful for the opportunity to say goodbye, and yet somehow I knew I truly wouldn't say goodbye for a long time after.

As I was assisted back into my hospital bed after I said my final goodbyes to Nathan, my mom and dad gave me some privacy as they went to visit in the waiting room down the hall. I sat in my bed and stared out the window trying to comprehend the weight of everything that transpired. My gaze shifted across the cards and flowers and gifts from so many that supported and loved me. Finally my eyes rested on the table tray next to my bed, to which the Gratitude Journal I received a few days earlier still lay. Unsure as to how to move forward, I knew I had to articulate my emotions somehow. I opened the journal up and found April 8 and wrote my first entry of daily gratitudes:

1. *That I got to spend two years of my life with Nathan.*
2. *That I experienced true love.*
3. *That I know he's in a better place*
4. *That God has a bigger plan for me.*
5. *That I survived.*

Recovery was a long and audacious process. Physically, I had to relearn how to walk again. Countless laps up and down the corridors were made, greeting the nurses and other patients making rounds.

"Way to go, girl! Looking good!" a nurse cheered as I unsteadily shuffled by the nurse's station.

"Atta girl, Kathryn!" cheered another.

In my mind, I could only think of how dumb this all was.

Learning how to walk, again? I know how to do this. Why can't my body just keep up? It felt more like an aggressive willpower carrying my feet than physical movement. I shuffled further. *Why am I so out of breath? Oh yeah, my lung.* Again forgetting the extent of my injuries, my frustrations mounted which almost instantaneously converted into more fierce determination. *The sooner I do this, the sooner I can get back to normal*, I thought.

Yet, I didn't know what normal was anymore. How does one start rebuilding a life they once knew when their entire world was shattered in just one day?

"You're doing great, Kathryn," my physical therapist encouraged. "This will be the last lap for the day."

"I can do one more," I replied eagerly. I so wanted to prove my ability and work ethic.

"Not today. You've done more than enough," he offered, reading my bluff. "Besides, I already know you're a fighter. You don't have to prove anything to me." As I hoisted myself back into the hospital bed, I realized how good it felt to rest. "The occupational therapist will be here shortly. Don't set the sky as the limit for them, either, okay? You are making great progress." I rolled my eyes. *But you're not the one stuck in here*, I thought.

Occupational Therapy was ridiculous in my mind, as I had to learn how to do common tasks like getting in and out of a car, showering, and proper alignment in sleeping. All of the seemingly miniscule tasks that we take for granted every single day, were now a chore. Even worse, they were hard. Little movements seemed monumental and taxing. Simple things like holding my arms up washing my hair, taking the stairs, and even talking too much exhausted me.

I was forced to wear my back brace all waking hours, with the only exception of showering and sleeping. I wasn't allowed to lock the bathroom door while I showered, as my mom stood outside of it in the event I fell, and she had to rescue me. I was out of school for over a month and had to build up stamina to even get to half days. Because I wasn't allowed to stay home alone, I got to go to back to my old babysitter's house, to which I loved! My days were filled with naps, playing with the little kids at her daycare, coloring, and snack time. Even getting ready in the morning gave me more of a purpose.

Finally, I was cleared to go to full days the last week of school, since they were basically slush days. Although everything was the same, everything had changed. My friends, classmates, and teachers were all excited to see me, yet something was different. I was treated as the super special girl, getting preferential treatment with my elevator pass, someone to carry my books and lunch tray, even a special cushioned chair to sit in. Yet, it was the look in everyone's eyes that gave it away. They no longer saw me as Kathryn. They saw me as the girl from the accident.

I know had a force field around me that no one dared penetrate, as I was portrayed as being as delicate as fine crystal. Ironic, as I had already withstood the strongest storm. I hadn't cracked yet, what made everyone think I was going to now?

● ● ●

I can't even remember who broke the news to me after the accident. I was still in deep denial that Nate could hurt me so badly by cheating, but then it got exponentially worse. Camila, the girl he cheated with, was pregnant. And even more so, she was excited about it. However, she wasn't sure if the baby was Nate's. I asked Bruce and Laurie if it was true. They promised me they were going to get to the bottom of things, as they were somewhat shocked at this revelation, as well. A paternity test was ordered; however it was not to be done until after the baby was born.

At school, Camila wasn't involved in anything and was very emo. She was short, plump and was the first girl among the class to develop breasts and get her period. Camila was very vocal about her escapades in high school but being the naive girl that I was (who did not know what drugs or sex was) I assumed she was a big talker because nobody actually does that sort of thing... especially at 15. I was a good, Catholic girl who was involved in activities, a cheerleader, blonde hair, blue green eyes, and a slim figure. Although I had a mouth with a fiery attitude, I was meek in experimenting with anything remotely dangerous as I was afraid it would get back to my mom and those consequences were too risky for the actual behavior. I was good enough to be arm candy and to engage in deep, philosophical conversations, but when it came to sex and my belief of waiting until marriage (or until I knew what the hell sex actually was), I wasn't good enough to wait for.

Why her? If we were so close and had such a strong connection, wouldn't you think sex would've been the next step between us? Didn't he know that by cheating, let alone lying and breaking a sacred promise would be the end of us? Did he somehow know that we were over and just said screw it? Was it just once or was it multiple times? Did he like it? Did he like her? Did he even think about me? All these thoughts swirled in my head.

From the moment I found out Nathan had cheated, she became nonexistent to me. The emotional reactions I had towards her only intensified once I found out the baby was his. A boy. And the Brown's lovingly extended grace and gave him their last name, and ultimately, their home. For years, I ignored this. I felt betrayed by his family who accepted her and this baby into their home, so I stopped reaching out. I didn't want to be a part of something so hurtful or wrong in my eyes. How could they love another girl and baby like they loved me? In my heart, I realized I was replaceable.

The accident was a soul fracture.

The baby? That became a soul lesson.

• • •

Kneeling down in my music teacher's small, cramped closet-sized office, I kept my eyes on the floor. I was surrounded by loose stacks of sheet music on the floor, her desk and on top of the already plum-full file cabinets. I'd been in there hundreds of times before and never noticed it, yet today, it symbolized how I felt inside. Scattered. Thrown about. No rhyme or reason to the organized chaos within. A year had passed since the accident.

"I don't know why I even applied," I said quietly, still looking down. "Who am I when so many others are way better than me? I'm just going to pull it."

"Kathryn," Mrs. Olafson said gently as she put her hand on my shoulder as she sat in her chair leaning forward to face me. "You are an amazing vocalist. You have grown into that incredibly big voice of yours and it is a sheer gift. This is a momentous time for you!"

I was quiet for a few moments. "Nobody even knows I applied. Not even my mom," I said, finally raising my eyes to catch her soft gaze. "I didn't want to get anyone's hopes up for when I don't make it."

"And what if you do make it?" she offered, speculating that I actually had a chance. "What if Juilliard sent a letter back and invited you to audition in-person?"

I smiled at the thought. "That would be amazing," I replied, quickly followed by a hard dose of reality. "But that won't happen. I've made up my mind, I'm pulling my application." My eyes brimmed with tears and my heart full of the familiar sadness that I've come to accept in it.

"Are you sure?" Mrs. Olafson asked one more time.

"I can't move away from here," I said as the tears finally fell. "Who am I to think I can traipse off to New York City from a town of a hundred people and compete for a coveted spot in one of the most prestigious art schools in the world?"

Mrs. Olafson handed me a tissue as I kept on, "And then what? Leave my mom? Leave all that I know for a silly dream? I can't dance. I can't act. My chances for making it on Broadway are one in a million. Even then, I can't even play the piano well enough to accompany anyone to even be a music teacher. I can only sing. That doesn't get me very far in life, so why bother? I'm just saving everyone the heartache now before they even knew I did something so stupid like apply to Juilliard."

She shushed and soothed me as I let the tears fall, not flinching a bit when the second bell rang, and I was officially late for my next class. "You have more than enough to give, my dear," she said quietly. "I don't think it's fair for you to give up on yourself before even hearing back. Your audition tape was amazing. *You* are amazing. You have competed at the state level and won... don't forget that. You were meant to be on stage and you know it." She took my hand and helped lift me up and then put her arms around me in a hug. "But if you are truly not ready and you've already made up your mind, then okay. I respect your decision to retract your application."

I had no words to respond back with. Just tears and a sense of defeat, yet relief knowing that I never had to tell a soul.

"I also want you to know, Kathryn," she continued, "that you are such a special young lady. All that you've been through, all that you have become... it's inspiring to think of where you will end up. If not Juilliard, then it will be even better. God has a special purpose for you, I hope you know that."

Wiping the tears away, I whispered, "Yeah." Everyone tells me that. *Hurry up, God, and reveal this Divine plan already. I'm sick of waiting. I survived for a reason, so show me and do something with what's left of this ragged soul.*

My heart was much too fragile, and I couldn't risk it breaking any more than it already was. I was still picking up the shattered pieces, even a year later. Questions plagued me of worthiness, deciding to play small, and stay safe in my comfortable, Midwestern life. I tried to deny the fact of being accepted into Juilliard, but that didn't deny the fact that I was Juilliard-quality.

I was living a life of brokenness every single day while pretending to be glued back together. I started layering masks to be who others thought I should be. I didn't want to grow up anymore. I had already done that and lived a thousand more lives by the age of 15 than anyone else I had known. I wanted simple. I wanted safe.

And yet, my soul begged for more.

Until I learned to realize my own worth, the universe would keep bringing me to the edge. Life was never going to be simple again.

chapter six

....

FREE BIRD

As we gingerly walked in the back door, the smell of stale smoke filled my nose and I heard crooning vocals ending a song. Aaron confidently walked in and I meekly followed, peeking around his massive 6' 4" build to see if I recognize anyone who would pose a problem. As with any small-town bar, when the door opens, everyone turns to see who it is. Not seeing anyone who important, we passed the bar and make our way to the booths and tables.

Being underage in the local bar always gave me butterflies in my stomach. Sure, it was illegal, but it's a small town and those who frequented the bar never really cared. But that quick panic of *what if someone recognizes us and tells my mom*? And yet, you just never knew. Mark's prominent size and demeanor took over his side of the booth, but as he saw us, his wide smile broadened, and his entire face lit up.

"Sister!" he called out. We neared the booth and he stood up to shake hands with Aaron and heartily joked, "What took you so long, man? Can't you get your piece of shit car to work before picking up my sister?"

"Nah, just got stuck in traffic," Aaron sarcastically replied with a big smile, knowing full well that we met one car on the road during the 12-mile drive to town.

"Haha! Right!" laughed Mark. "Whatchya drinking tonight?"

Both Aaron and I looked nervously at each other, not saying a word. Knowing full well that we were underage, Mark reassured us. "It's fine. It's just Chubbs and she don't care. She knows you're with me." I graduated high school over a year ago and was just finishing up beauty school while Aaron just graduated from technical school. Nobody knew him, and he looked way older than nineteen, but I wasn't so sure that I couldn't be more recognizable, even with shades of pink gracing my long, blonde hair.

My neighbor and fellow hairstylist Wendy came from the stage and gave me a huge hug. "You ready to sing, girl?" she asked, referring to karaoke, where she just put in her name for another song. Wendy was married and had kids, but she was always up for a good time, and anytime there was karaoke, she was ready to sing. She and Mark loved doing duets together.

"Maybe. What songs are you doing tonight?" I replied.

"A little bit of this, and a little bit of that," Wendy said with a wink. "You know me, give me all the '80s! I saved the big ones for you, though!"

"Ha, thanks," I said. "We'll see what I feel in the mood for."

The petite waitress came over. Her curly red hair was wild and big, just like her personality, which seemed double of her small frame.

"Chubbs!" Mark exclaimed, holding his Coors Light. "We'll take a round!"

"They're not drinking," she replied, matter-of-factly.

"What? She's cool, promise," Mark tried persuading with his usual charm.

"Not tonight," Chubbs said, putting her foot down.

"They're just here to sing. She's really good," he nodded at me. "Chubbs, you know she is." I just sat there wide-eyed, hoping not to get kicked out or worse, have word get back to my mom that I got kicked out of the bar now that it's been known who I am.

"She can sing, but they're not drinking." Chubbs replied, then turned to me with a smile. "You want a pop or something, hun?"

"Yes, please," I said. *Caught*, I thought. *But I still get to sing.*

She walked away with our order and Mark leaned over and said, "Don't worry, I'll take care of this. You're fine," insinuating that he would get us some beer as he followed Chubbs up to the bar to sweet talk her some more. I looked around now that I felt safe in my booth under the protection of my brother, to see who actually showed up for karaoke.

"Who's that?" I'd ask every time someone got up to sing, as I didn't recognize the crowd that usually hung out at the bar, since I never actually went to the bar at nineteen.

"Nobody you know," Mark said. "They're older than mom and dad, but they always show up to sing."

"Trying to sing, you mean," I quipped. I found myself mighty judgmental critiquing vocals and song selection based on their range and style. I was a classically-trained operetta singer, having taken over seven years of vocal lessons at that point and singing in front of thousands of people, so I felt as if I was some hot shit coming back to a bunch of townies singing crappy karaoke. Instead, I just patiently paged through the books of songs as I waited my turn to show them what real singing actually sounded like.

"You know, you missed Mark singing a really good song," Wendy commented as Mark was gone.

"What? Which one?" I asked, knowing his repertoire and usual song selections.

"He was brave tonight," she said. "He did *Free Bird*, and it was ah-mazing! Seriously, you missed probably the best he's ever sang before. You walked in probably five minutes after he got done, and that's the first thing he said, *"Dammit, she missed it!"*

"Awwww!" I pouted. "That sucks." My heart panged with bittersweetness. As sad as I was that I missed his song, I loved hearing how much Mark wanted me to see him in his glory, truly standing in the spotlight and only having me, his kid sister, look up at him with beaming pride, just as he always did when I sang.

"I think I just saw him sign up for it again, so I think you'll get round two!" Wendy winked. "Just for you."

Mark came back with another round of beer for all of us. "Told you I'd take care of you!"

"Eh, I don't think I should. I feel bad," I said, as Aaron grabbed a beer and took a swig.

Mark beamed at him, "Atta boy! I knew I liked you!" Mark then turned to me, "Have you found a song yet?"

"I've got a couple up there! Some Jo Dee Messina, Sara Evans, and Pat Benetar, of course, "I replied. "What can I sign you up for?"

"Surprise me. You know what I like," Mark said.

"Good. Because I already did," I laughingly said. "You and Timmy O. are doing *Beer for My Horses*."

Mark beamed as he raised his bottle, "Hell yeah, we are! I'll go tell him right now!" and just like that, he left to make his way back to the bar where a crowd was gathering for the night. 10:30

pm seemed to be the magic hour that people actually made their way downtown. For a small town like Fertile, population 780, it had three bars. The Sandhill, which was at the edge of town and was a bar, restaurant, and drive in which most young people frequented. The Legion was more for the older vets, and the Other Place was for all the others that didn't quite fit. I had never been in the other two, as I had no reason to, Mark would tell me. *"Nothing for you there,"* he'd say.

He was a social butterfly, chatting it up with anyone and everyone who came into the bar. His charisma and charm were contagious and was known as a *Goodtime Charlie* and someone who often had the party continue well after the bar closed at his house, which resided on our family farm. Mark's parties were known to be loud, lively, and always a good time. *I wouldn't be surprised if he doesn't extend that offer tonight, too*, I thought.

Another singer finished up their song, and people clapped. Soon it was my turn, and Mark led the group in cheering as I got up on stage. When the song started, I could hear Mark saying, "Shhhh! My sister's singing! You listen, now!" I belted out Pat Benetar's *Hit Me With Your Best Shot* and loved the energy and attention of holding a microphone and the way the air was magnetic. It was my three minutes of fame, being the center of attention and knowing that Aaron and Mark's eyes were all on me. They were my two favorite people; my brother and my heart. As the last notes faded, Mark led the crowd in whooping and hollering my praises, and my face turns a shade of red from the over-the-top embarrassment. But he didn't care; he would enthusiastically exclaim, "That's my sister!" to anyone who would listen.

Mark joined me back at the booth and sang my praises even more, this time to Aaron. "Did you hear her?" he exclaimed, with a wide grin and wild eyes. "Did you *hear* her?"

Aaron and put his arm around me for a squeeze. He pushed his face into my hair to kiss the side of my head.

"Good one," he said quietly into my ear. Aaron was deceiving with his big stature. Towering inches over Mark, Aaron was very subdued and quiet versus Mark's gregarious nature. Aaron is an observer and loves to soak everything in and is not one to be in the limelight.

• • •

The four of us, Mark, Wendy, Aaron, and I, continued to chat while the next names were called to sing. As there were some playful bantering between us, Wendy smiled and joked, "I can't believe I knew you two as little babes all those years ago sitting in the pews at church! And here you are!" referring to Aaron and me. "Who would've thought childhood friends would lead to this?"

I leaned into him and smiled, "It is sweet, isn't it? It's a good thing I stole those movie tickets from you all those years ago!" Aaron smiled, raised his beer to lips and responded, "Mmmhmm."

I laughed and asked, "Well, I wasn't going to wait around forever, you know! Tell me, how long would it have taken you to ask me out?"

Aaron teased back, "Years."

Silently, I knew that he was right. That sweet, quiet, shy boy from my confirmation class who always sat in the pew in front of us at church hardly said a word. How in the world would he have ever gotten the courage to ask me on a date? In true Kathryn fashion, I asked him out on our first date when we were 15, just six weeks after the accident. There we were, four years later, and he was my rock. The boy who saw passed a broken girl wearing a back brace, helped me carry my emotional heartbreak when it was too heavy to do so alone, and become my anchor in the unsteady waters as I splashed around trying to find my way. I squeezed

Aaron's big hand and smiled as I soaked in his dark, handsome features.

"Next up we have Mark!" the DJ announced. "Mark, please make your way to the stage." The stage was nothing more than a step up strategically placed in the corner of the bar where no more than a four-person band could fit, but still, it was just what we needed to be a karaoke star.

The music cues up and the guitar solo starts; tears immediately started swelling in my eyes.

I patted Aaron's hand excitedly, exclaiming, "This is it!" and fixed my gaze back on Mark. As he crooned the sweet melody of the first verse of *Free Bird* by Lynard Skynard, I mouthed the words right along with him, sitting on the edge of my seat. It felt as if he and I were the only ones in the bar and immediately I knew exactly what Wendy had meant. There was something special about this song and Mark singing it. I was completely entranced and by the time the song had ended, ten minutes later, I laughed because only Mark could get away with picking a long-ass song like *Free Bird*.

The bar cheered, but I don't know if it was because the song was finally over or if Mark was the highlight of the night, but either way, I had never been more connected to Mark. We finally had transitioned from the big brother, little sister paradigm that we had always known and were equals.

• • •

Two days after Christmas, my cell phone rang at 2:30 a.m. The TV was still on, but was an empty, static screen as the movie I fell asleep to was over. I got into the habit of falling asleep to the television to drown out the silence of living alone in my two-bedroom apartment. I had just made it back to my apartment from my parent's house less than five hours beforehand.

Mom and Dad's name flashed on my caller ID, to which I groggily answered, "Hello?"

"Babe?" my mom answered.

"Yeah?" I said, still half asleep.

"Babe, there's been an accident," my mom said calmly. "It's Mark. He's been in an accident. They are taking him to Crookston, you better come. It doesn't look good."

"Okay," I responded, still not comprehending what was going on. I climbed out of bed and slip on my shoes and coat. I didn't bother getting dressed knowing full well I'd be coming back home and crawling into bed in a few hours.

I drove my little blue Geo Prizm through town and out on the highway and started to wake up. *Doesn't look good*, I thought, staring out onto the road. Not a headlight was in sight. *What does that mean...doesn't look good? I broke my back and I'm fine*, I thought. *Pete broke his neck, and even though he had a halo for months, he's fine*, I reassured myself. They have the technology to fix broken bones these days. I know a lot of people in car accidents and they are fine after they get fixed up. I continued to drive the 20 miles to the hospital where my mom told me to meet.

When I entered the emergency room, my brother Matt was standing there, looking out the window, surely waiting for me. "Mom's that way," he said, pointing down the hall. Not questioning my brother, a man with few words ever, I scooted down the hall a little faster just to meet my mom coming out of a room. Her eyes were red, and she was shaking. I saw my dad out of the corner of my eye, pacing back and forth, hands in pockets, staring at the ground.

"What? What is it? Is he alright?" I asked.

"Babe…" my mom broke off, starting to cry again. "He's gone."

I stared at her, gauging this cruel joke she just bestowed on me. I backed against the wall and started shaking my head, "No. No, no, no. NO!"

Down the hall, Matt stared out the window; my dad paced the other end frantically. I slid down the wall to the floor and wrapped my arms around my legs and pressed my knees into my eyes to keep them from watering. I lifted my head to the bright hospital lights, trying to connect to God. "No! This can't happen. He can't leave me. You can't do this to me AGAIN!" I started sobbing uncontrollably. My mom knelt down to try to comfort me, but I was too far gone. My hysterical blubbering, crying out, and wailing filled the empty hallways of the emergency room, another stark reminder of what remained of my heart.

I couldn't even pull myself together to call and tell anyone, plus it was the middle of the night. It wasn't until Aaron called me hours later in the morning that I realized the one person who I needed the most I let slip my mind.

• • •

The days that followed were a blur. I, however, pulled myself together to become the fixer. My strength had always been finding calm among the chaos, so I went to work. My dad took Mark's death hard, but as a man of little words, he buried himself in his work at the farm. He wanted to be alone and I know the reprieve of doing something with his hands idled his mind. My mom, however, broke down, rightfully so. Losing a child is nothing anyone should ever experience, and her worst nightmare had come true. Matt took after my dad and engulfed himself in busywork. He honored Mark by welding a cross with his name on it and placed it in the field where they found Mark's body.

At just 19 years old, I wrote my 23-year-old brother's obituary. I went through all of the pictures and created montages to celebrate Mark's life. I worked with the same funeral director who buried Nathan to help coordinate Mark's last wishes. An oak casket with deer plates mounted to the side, a tribute to Mark's nickname, "Buck." Songs to be sung at his funeral. The shirt he was buried in, I picked out, washed, and pressed. I did it all for him, my hero.

I was no stranger to grief, but this time it felt different. Peaceful, almost. As if Mark knew I had already had enough heartache, he tried to make it easier from the other side. Yet grief is a tricky and elusive thing. It doesn't come in a straight line and although I thought I knew the worst kind of heartbreak, I wasn't prepared for a double whammy. Emotions that I had stuffed just a short three years earlier rose within me. It wasn't anger that Mark was gone, but it was intense anger that I had to go through it again. *I already did this.*

The night before Mark's funeral, after the visitation, I hit a wall. We had family at the house celebrating Mark's life together and I was slowly dying inside. All of the stories and laughter and tears that were shared from everyone seemed to offset the heartbreak that everyone was feeling, except for me. I couldn't breathe, the grief was so heavy sitting on my chest. I couldn't take it any longer.

"This is bullshit," I muttered. "I just can't," I said as I stood up from the couch and walked out of the room. I needed someplace to go, but it was now January and we had a house full of people, so spare room was limited. I found myself in the laundry room, on the floor up against the washer and dryer, again sobbing uncontrollably. Since our house was a ranch farmhouse, my crying echoed naturally, putting a damper on the love being shared by everyone in the other room. My mom came to check on me, kneeling down close and rubbing my back. "I shouldn't be here. I don't want to be here!" My body shaking violently against the washer and dryer set. "I want to be with him! I don't want to be here!"

"Shhh," she whispered, wiping my tears. "I know it's not fair. But we have to keep going." I just shook my head, unable to respond to that. I didn't want to keep going. I wanted to go back to the way things were. I wanted my brother back.

After a bit, my mom got up and Aaron came into the laundry room, presumably because my mom told him to come in and calm me down. He sat down next to me, back against the dryer and I collapsed into his lap, still sobbing. "I don't want to be here anymore! I just want to be with him!"

Trying to understand, Aaron calmly asked, "Kathryn, do you really want to die?"

The weight of those word consumed me, bringing me back to the severity and fragility of life. I sat up and looked at his sweet dark eyes that were searching mine for the truth.

I struggled to breathe. "I...just...don't...want...to...hurt... anymore." To that he didn't say a word, but he didn't need to. His presence of just being there helped me fall apart, knowing I was safe to do so because he was there to pick up the pieces, just like he did after my accident.

• • •

Burying my brother what seemed like right after burying my best friend felt like a one-two punch to the heart. A double-edged sword that twisted a teeny bit each passing day. Just being 19 and having lived a thousand lives in just a few short years seemed insurmountable.

"What am I doing with my life?" I sobbed to Aaron one night, after feeling the weight of the world press down on me. "How were these beautiful, rich lives taken so soon and here I am, desperately trying to figure out what God's purpose?"

"You can do or be anything, Kathryn," Aaron said quietly as he brushed my matted hair out of my face. After a few moments he offered, "Maybe your purpose is to keep going."

"Doing what?" I charged through angry, hot tears. "Being stuck in a mindless job as a hairstylist? Doing something I'm good at, but something I clearly don't love? It's a paycheck. I invest in my clients. But no one invests in me."

"I believe in you," he whispered, barely audible as he continued to smooth my hair. The love and admiration of someone investing in me. He didn't know it at the time, but him holding space for me to break down, breathe, and regroup was exactly what I needed.

Thankfully, my faith in God and a higher purpose kept me putting one foot in front of the other. Two huge lessons in grieving two of the biggest influencers in my life propelled me on an epic search of where I belonged. I perceived myself being known as "the girl who lost everything" and I saw pity everywhere. Refusing to let Mark's and Nathan's deaths be a defining point of my life, I was committed to making something of myself. I wanted to be known for something I did rather than what happened to me.

I connected to my higher truth like I did in that Mighty Oak so very long ago. Finding God within myself to find my place in the world where He required me to serve others was my mission. And yet, I had no idea how that looked. Mark's death elevated me and empowered me to push harder, to stretch further, and to soar higher than I ever dreamed. I knew deep down that again, I was made for more and settling was not going to be an option.

Even though I was a stylist for less than a year, my coworkers had become family to me, especially after Mark died. That spring, the salon manager found out she was pregnant and was already planning for her future with the salon. After the last salon meeting, she had stayed after and we chatted about me possibly taking over as manager when she went on maternity leave. The key would be that I would take on the assistant manager position and learn the ropes, and then move seamlessly into the manager role and stay there come December.

A new leadership role sounded enticing to me, like a total step up. Salon Manager at the age of 20. Yet, something was holding me back. I told her that I'd have to think about it.

On a Saturday in late June, I was starting a full-head color with a client. The salon was busy for a Saturday and everyone was buzzing about gearing up for the Fourth of July holiday weekend coming up. A regular to the salon, my client knew and chatted with the other stylists. My station was nestled between Sadie and Ellen. Somehow we got to discussing upcoming holidays, birthdays, and anniversaries.

"Well you know," started Sadie. "July is a big month for Ellen and I." She continued with her haircut as she talked excitedly. "I will be celebrating 18 years as a stylist, and Ellen will be celebrating 20!"

"What?!" I exclaimed, along with our clients. "That's huge!"

"I bet you've been cutting my hair for 17 of those 18 years," replied her client from the chair.

Sadie laughed, "I bet I have!"

Ellen chimed in from the other side of me, "You know, Kat. Never in a million years did I think that I'd make it 20 years as a stylist. This was never going to be my full-time job and look where we're at! Twenty years flies by before you know it!"

I smiled and continued on with applying the dark, rich color to my client's roots. Inside that comment sunk in deep and hard. I was trying hard to keep my horrified facial expressions to a minimum. *Twenty years. TWENTY YEARS. Doing hair for twenty years seems like an eternity, I thought, almost dizzy. There is no way in hell that I want to be doing this, THIS, in twenty years.* The thought of being a 20-year-old manager flashed to being a 40-year-old manager in the same salon. Counting inventory, managing schedules, training young and inexperienced stylists. *No. No. Hell no.*

The conversation swirled in my head for the rest of the day, in and out for the next few weeks until I talked to Sadie about the assistant manager position as we were closing up alone on our scheduled Thursday nights together.

"I can't be your assistant manager," I confessed as I was cleaning up my station, knowing how disappointed she was going to be. "Sade, I just can't. The thought of me being 20 and managing the salon is both humbling and terrifying. I truly appreciate you asking me, but I can't."

"Kat, you would be amazing. The leadership that you'll gain will be worth it and I promise you, I'll set you up for complete success while I'm gone. And I'm only a phone call away if you need me," Sadie said, trying to persuade me.

"No, I really can't," I replied. "I have gone back and forth with this and as we celebrate yours and Ellen's anniversaries next week, it's really hitting home. I went to UND this morning to ask about admissions."

Sadie stopped and turned to me, "You did what?!" Her shock turned to genuine excitement almost instantly. "That's incredible!"

I laughed. "I mean, I still have to apply, and I still have to get accepted, but there's a caveat for me to take up 12 credits as a Non-Degree Seeking Student, which I would have to be until I take my ACTs. I never took them in high school since I didn't think I'd ever go to college."

Sadie came around her chair and gave me a big hug, "I am so

proud of you! This is awesome! I mean, not for me because I'll have to find someone else as assistant manager, but awesome for you because this is the real thing! And this is the perfect job while you go to school. Flexibility in-between classes and hardly any late nights! Seriously, Kat. This is awesome."

I smiled as I felt her genuine excitement for me. "After Mark died, I've had this feeling of *more* creeping in these past few months. Like, I was made for more. I thought maybe it was as a manager or educator, but I wasn't sure. And then when you brought up yours and Ellen's anniversaries that one Saturday, it was like a truck hit me. I had supper with my mentor on Monday and had my appointment with admissions today. It's been a whirlwind."

She went back to her station and continued to clean up while I walked up front to cash out the register. A few moments later, Sadie said, "You know, I knew I had a feeling when I hired you that I'd have to give you up eventually."

I turned around and faced her, "What?"

"I knew you weren't going to be here forever," she turned to me and said matter-of-factly. "I had a feeling once I knew how special and wonderful you are, that this wasn't going to be all for you. I just tried to ignore that and keep you to myself for as long as I could." She smiled from the back of the salon.

I laughed and turned back to finish the register. The thought of spreading my wings and still having the stability of familiarity felt right. "Don't worry," I joked. "You're not getting rid of me just yet."

"I am not afraid;
I was born to do this."

– St. Joan of Arc

chapter seven

....

LOST

As I walked the long trek across the University of North Dakota campus from the parking lot to the Student Union, I gritted my teeth and tensed up as the damp, raw wind blew right through my jacket. I dug my hands further into my pockets and listened to my feet crunch steadily through the snow as the December temperature was hovering around 10 degrees but felt like -5 degrees with the strong wind chill. With barely any trees and zero hills to block the wind, the streets of campus between the large buildings and massive trees became a glorified wind tunnel and walking to class felt treacherous. I hurried my step even faster and felt the sweet relief of warmth inside.

The Union was buzzing, which was surprising for a Thursday afternoon. *Everyone's group projects are in full swing*, I thought. I walked past the crowded food court of students chatting, studying, and eating to stop into the Student Involvement Office to visit my sorority sister, Lucy, who worked there. I was early for my meeting, so I made myself at home at the table next to the desk and waited for her to finish helping some presumably poor, unfortunate freshman soul who was questioning the different options of student involvement related to Fisheries and Wildlife. *None*, I thought sarcastically, yet admiring Lucy's patience and ability to keep a straight face. *Pick a different major or find a new hobby, kid.*

Lucy winked at me as the guy asked his last question before

walking off with some pamphlets. Lucy turned and flashed her white teeth to me in a smile. "Webs! Hi!"

"Hey girl, how's it going?" I asked.

"Good, but boring today," Lucy replied. "Where you off to?"

"I've got my group project to finish up. It's the really big one that counts for most of my grade, but it's also for that client I was telling you about," I explained. Our Public Relations class was split into groups working on actual PR campaigns for clients in the community and the winning campaign will get launched in the new year for said client. "My group stinks and I've done most of the work, but it's still good and at least I know it'll be legit."

"You always get stuck with lame groupies!" she said. "Maybe your professors know you'll always help the underdog do better?"

"Maybe. Or maybe they pick me because they know I'll do it all," I shoot back, half joking, half wondering if it's true.

"You ready for tonight?" Lucy asked, talking about the much-anticipated concert that was set for the night.

"Just this meeting, closing the shop, and then I'll be over to get ready!" I said excitedly. "I wish I could've gotten someone to cover, but it's only until 8 p.m., and the band doesn't even start until 9 p.m., so there will be plenty of time for pre-partying."

"Oh geez, of course you'll make plenty of time," Lucy said sarcastically. "Is Samantha going with you?"

"Yeah, I'll have to find out what time she plans on getting to town," I said. "You'll still do my makeup for me? Hopefully it'll be quiet in the shop, so I can do my hair there. I think I'm booked, but maybe someone will cancel."

"Absolutely! I have a new palette I want to try out on you," she explained. "Lots of golds and shimmers, which always look great on you!"

"Awesome," I said, checking the time. "Gotta run. Maybe someone will surprise me and beat me to the room."

"Probably not, knowing your groupie luck," Lucy laughed. "See you after work!"

"Bye, love," I waved as I walked out the door and down the hall.

• • •

I made a quick stop at the coffee shop to get my usual, a sugar-free caramel latte, extra hot. *Something to get me through the next hour of hell*, I thought as I walked up the staircase to meet my group in a meeting room. *Lucy is right, I do get stuck with the sucky groups.*

I opened up the door to find I was the first to arrive, per usual. I set my backpack down, pulled out my laptop, folders, and planner. Checking the time, I tried not to get fidgety as the time neared closer and closer to 3:30 p.m. Knowing that I had limited time to make this happen before I had to be at work by 4:45 p.m., I prayed that everyone would show up on time and make this quick and painless, so I wasn't late for work. *Hell, I did it all, we just need to finalize the presentation and they need to send their portions of the paper to me to assemble*, I thought. *An hour will be plenty of time.*

One-by-one, my group members trickled in and by 3:35 p.m. all were present. We didn't have time to waste, so we all dove right in, with me at the helm. A natural leader, delegation has always been a strong point, along with making cohesion out of chaos. We worked seamlessly together, blending our ideas and themes into one to create a rocking presentation to supplement our already dynamic paper.

"Alright guys, I've got five minutes before I have to go," I said. "Anything else we need to cover? I'm feeling really good about this PR campaign we came up with!"

"We have the best one by far," commented Caroline. "My roommate's group can't get their shit together and I believe she said they haven't even started their paper yet."

"Yikes," another group member said as we all made faces reacting to that other group's progress.

"We will knock it out of the park, I can feel it," I said as I started putting my things back into my bag. "I will have the paper finalized this weekend and will send both the paper and PowerPoint to you all to keep for your portfolios."

"Great, sounds good," Caroline said. "Thanks for your work on this."

"Not a problem," I replied. "I want us to win this campaign. It's really good. The client is going to be so excited! See you all next week!" *Finally. Let's get this show on the road.*

• • •

Thankfully, the salon was slow and steady that night. I was booked with two haircuts and a color, so my night flew by. All my regular clients, I chatted effortlessly and caught up on the busyness of their lives. Sitting there listening to my dear friend who just got married, I was so thankful that I had gone to beauty school after high school. So even as a full-time college student enrolled at the university and majoring in communications, I was able to work my way through college at a job that I enjoyed fulfilling my creativity and connecting with clients who became my friends. After doing hair for six years, I had built up a reputable clientele that supported me and my dream of being a professional speaker.

As I pulled up to my sorority house, I grabbed my bag to change and made sure the cooler hadn't spilled in my trunk. Our sorority was a dry house, meaning no alcohol on the premises, but the frat next door wasn't, so we could always go over there for a couple of drinks before heading to the bar.

I walked in and head upstairs to Lucy's room, where I usually crashed when going out with the girls. Since I lived a couple of miles off of campus alone, it was easier to get a ride back to the house with everyone else versus finding my own ride home. I met Lucy in the hall, and she said, "I saved you a late plate. Want me to grab it for you?"

"Oh, thank you! Yes, please!" I replied, relieved that she was thinking of me. Late plates were hot meals reserved for those who miss supper at the house, instead of eating plain sandwiches. Lucy knew me and how I needed to eat before a night of heavy drinking.

I started getting dressed into my other clothes, noticing the drastic difference between the plain black pants and ugly dress shirt under my smock. The tight, bootcut jeans and low-cut v-top that showed off my perky, voluminous breasts that were the focal point of my outfit. My big hair already done and subtle, yet shimmery make up about to be applied, I assessed myself in the mirror. *Not bad*, I thought. *I wish I was more toned, but I'll definitely get on stage tonight.*

"Whoa, mama!" Lucy ogled as she walked in with my plate of food.

"You look HOT!"

"Think so?" I asked, needing the confirmation to feed my confidence and mask my insecurity. Pulling my shirt down for a bit more cleavage, "I can only work with what I've got!"

"Love it. You're so lucky! I love that top on you and the way your boobs look!" she replied, already ready to go out. "What time is Samantha getting to town?"

"She said 9:30, which really means like 10:00," I sighed. No sense of time was one of my biggest pet peeves, as I am a stickler for being early. Plus, if there is a band and only a few hours of drinking time, you best bet I was going to maximize the most out of it.

"Eat," Lucy said, putting the plate in front of me, "I'll do your make up."

"Thanks, love. It stinks you can't go out with me tonight," I said, acknowledging Lucy was still underage.

"Nah, you go have fun. Molly and I are headed next door to party with Ricky and the boys," she responded, talking about our favored fraternity on campus. "You'll come with for a bit before you head out?"

"I have the cooler packed, already!" I replied, smiling.

"Are you crashing here? My bed is ready for you," Lucy said. "Or is the mister coming to pick you up?" Mister was my nickname for Aaron.

"We'll see. Depends on if there's an after party or maybe we'll hit the truck stop for breakfast," I said nonchalantly. "But Aaron isn't coming to town. He's much too responsible working early mornings. Plus, you know me, I always make my way home somehow!"

"You always do," Lucy replied, with a slight disapproving tone. I knew she wasn't a huge fan of Samantha, so I tried to ignore it, yet it still stung. How could my best friend not like my other best friend? I chalked it up to different spots in life, as Lucy was eyeball deep in her intense nursing program, whereas Samantha finished school already and was no stranger to going to her random jobs hung over. However, I knew it was deeper than that. Lucy knew me inside and out and was willing to love me through any chapter I was in, even if it meant me in a drunken stupor most nights versus the high-achieving and driven person during the day.

Hanging out with Samantha made me feel alive; the exact opposite of what I usually felt which was drowning in control and emotional upheaval. She was everything I wanted to be: carefree, unabashed at life, no real commitments or ties to anything, and her schedule revolved around various intramural sports which also included a cooler full of beer and a team of partiers. Her wild, dark, curly hair matched her spirit: untamed and unbroken. Something I craved; as it was something I was not.

• • •

The Johnny Holmes Band was one of my favorites to go to, as they were always a blast to rock out to. Plus, it was no secret that of my two years of following them that I was almost always sure to get on stage and sing with them.

"Need another?" asked Samantha, reaching out to grab my Coors Light bottle to check how much I had left.

"Yep!" I replied, just reveling in the weightlessness that always followed when I drank. All of the heavy and baggage that I was used to carrying somehow disappeared and I loved that feeling. I loved the invincible feeling that beer gave me; able to be the daring, flirty girl who sang and danced on stage, ready for anything. I was careful not to drink hard alcohol because I hated piecing the night back together, and I was able to control myself with beer. I knew my limits, or at least that's what I told myself.

I followed Samantha to the bar where we waited in line for another drink. The band was on break, so everyone else had the same idea. I found other friends to chat with and found the lead singer of the band across the bar. With all the liquid courage I had,

I marched right on up and swung my arm over his shoulder.

"Hey, you!" he said as he recognized who I was. "I wondered if you'd be here tonight! You having a good time?"

"Absolutely! You know I wouldn't have missed it!" I exclaimed.

"You need any extra vocals tonight? I'm ready if you are!"

"Maybe!" he yelled over the roar of people around us. "Come in the front and if we need you, I'll find you!"

"Done!" I smiled. "See you soon!" Someone else had grabbed his attention and I practically skipped back to the bar to find Samantha holding two more beers for me. "I'm in!" I said excitedly.

"I knew you would be!" she exclaimed. "Let's drink!"

When I got home that night, I pounded water and passed out. I woke the next morning with my usual glass and ibuprofen on my nightstand waiting for me. I was so used to the routine of getting myself up and coherent for class or work, it was like a ritual at this point. *Drink, eat shitty fast food to try to sober up, drive home, take out contacts, get water and ibuprofen, pass out.* I had to get to class as we were working on another project for finals. I threw on jeans and a sweatshirt, put my hair in a pony and ate some cheerios. Same hangover routine, different day. *I'll be fine by noon*, I thought, looking at the clock that read 9:25 a.m. *I need to be, at least. Hockey game is tonight, and those beers aren't going to drink themselves!*

• • •

Not even two weeks later during Christmas break, I found myself in the back of the police car, unable to comprehend what was actually happening. *This isn't happening*, I thought to myself. *I'm not like those who get arrested for drinking and driving. Those are people who are drunks and don't know any better.*

Only I *was* one of those people. I had been drinking for over 10 hours and I was pulled over for signaling that I was turning left when I decided to change lanes to the right. A cruiser was coming around the block and saw my erratic signaling and rightfully investigated.

In my rebellious independence, I was fiercely protective of never getting into a car with someone who had been drinking. However, I had a horrible habit of driving myself home every night so that I wouldn't find myself in an uncomfortable situation by crashing at someone else's place that I didn't fully trust.

In my fucked-up logic and even more horrid control, I assumed that if I was going to die, it was going to be at my own hands, not anyone else's. Not even thinking further down the line that I could ultimately take another person's life. I was so conditioned to believe that I could always be in control, even while my life was spiraling out of it.

But here I was, handcuffed in the back of the police cruiser after failing three sobriety tests, having heard my Miranda Rights, yet unable to fathom why me. I watched Samantha on the phone outside of the car I just vacated and the officer making sure she had a ride home. My head swirling, I was jarred when the dispatch went off asking about my arrival to County. My eyes glazed over the different lights flashing in the front seat, past the mounted rifle, and I saw my license on the officer's computer screen. All of this through the barricade that kept the officer safe from the criminal, only now I am the criminal.

The ride was quiet and short through town. As we arrived to the county jail, the large overhead door opened and closed behind us. The officer opened my door and escorted me into the small booking room, where he handed me off to the jailer.

"Is there anyone you'd like to call?" the female jailer asked.

"Lawyer? Parents?"

"I don't know, should I be?" I tearfully asked. "What do I do?"

"You have the right to call an attorney," she replied back in an automatic tone, probably used to dealing with two sides of the spectrum of drunks: tearful ones who have no clue of what to do or outrageously defiant ones. "There's a list of names and numbers if you'd like to contest your ticket."

"No, I did it," I responded. "Besides, I don't have any money to hire one."

Which is true. A broke college student who is already drowning in student loans didn't need to add on another hefty bill just to plead guilty anyway. The jailer started taking my fingerprints. Her hands were cold, and I tried to look her in the eyes to see what she saw. Finally, I interrupted her work by asking, "Do you think I'll be published in the *Fertile Journal* in the Court Proceedings? Like, will they publish my name?" Knowing full well that everyone reads those to keep up on the small-town gossip mill.

She didn't even flinch or look up as she kept marking each of my fingers with black ink and placing each one on my new record calmly and said, "Probably."

The hot tears ran down my face even harder. It's one thing to get a DUI in another town where nobody knew me, I could handle and ignore that. But the thought of having my mom feel the humiliation of reading my name in the local paper just as everyone else in town did under the court proceedings? The shame was real.

She finished up marking all ten fingers and taking a mouth swab, then an officer came over to explain all of the charges to me. I sat there not sure where to keep my eyes, so I transitioned from looking him in the eyes to staring at my hands. Unable to say anything back, I just tried to keep my composure and soak in my new reality. *Driving under the influence and failure to maintain control of the car. Fourteen hours of incarceration. Day and time of my court hearing.*

Once he was done, he stood up to go back out on patrol and the jailer came back over. "Can I call my fiancé?" I asked her. "Can I tell him what's going on?"

"Yes, the phone is over there. You have five minutes," she said.

I scurried over to the phone and started dialing Aaron's number. He picked up on the first ring. "Mister?" I cried into the phone. "I'm so sorry!"

"I know," he replied.

"You know?" I asked. "How?"

"Samantha," he said. "She called me to see if I could post bail for you as they wouldn't let her do it."

"Can you?" I asked hopeful.

"No, they say you have to remain there overnight," Aaron replied. "I don't know why, but that's what they said on the phone."

The silence between us was thick and deep, as we faced the reality of what was happening. I squeezed my eyes closed trying to stop the tears. "I don't have a car."

"I'll be there to pick you up tomorrow," he said. "You just sleep. I'll see you tomorrow."

I glanced at the jailer who signaled that my time was up. "I've got to go, Mister," I said. "I'm so sorry. I am just so sorry."

"I know. I love you," Aaron replied.

"I love you, too," I said as I hung up the phone. I turned back to the jailer and she motioned me over to the camera. It was time for my mug shot. Then the jailer walked me down the hall and stopped at a massive metal door. The drunk tank.

"No…" a guttural moan escaped my mouth, realizing what was happening. I started pleading with her, hoping that there was a shred of humanity in her being for an honest mistake that a young girl made. "No, no, no! I'm not a drunk! This is a mistake! I promise, I'm not like this!"

"I'm sorry, but I have to," she said as she finally looked me in the eyes, so I could see the first bit of remorse for my situation. "We are full tonight and it is standard protocol."

"I have to stay in here all night?" I questioned. A buzz sounded in the little hallway and the metal door unlocked of a private cell opened in front of me. The stench of previous drunks hit me as I took three steps into my new surroundings. I turned around just as the buzzer sounded again and the door slid shut. It looked and felt like solitary confinement.

My new reality.

Thoughts and scenarios ravaged my brain as I sat down on that cold slab of metal that jutted out from the wall. It looked like a bench that was supposed to be a bed, yet the mattress was gone. This was definitely solitary confinement. This wasn't supposed to be me.

And yet, how strange to have found myself in a small, metal cage yet again. Thoughts rattling around in my head, followed by sobbing and violent shivering. *Oh my God. Mom. How will I ever be able to tell my mom? She's going to read my name among the other arrests in the newspapers. She's going to be the subject of small town gossip. I've tainted her picture-perfect ideal. I'm such a disappointment for her. And Aaron! How in the world would he want to marry me now? Marrying such a sad, pathetic being. Six months before our wedding and I go and fuck it all up. Everything I've worked so hard for is completely shattered. I'm so ashamed at who I've become. I don't even know this person anymore.*

That was true. I didn't know who I was anymore. I was trying so hard to run from the fire that started years ago and the flames finally caught up and ultimately engulfed me. At the ripe old age of 23, I was the exact same age as my brother when he died. Actually, it was a mere five days before the anniversary of his death. My life in a complete downward spiral, at the same age as he was when it was tragically taken away. In that cell, I found myself going through the Stages of Grief of what I was going through: Denial, Anger, Bargaining, Depression, Acceptance.

The entire intake process was denial for me. I was not a criminal. I was not like the other drunks that they arrest. I was different. I knew better. It was a mistake. *A very horrible mistake that will never happen again, don't they know that? I don't belong here.*

But as I was sitting in the drunk tank, it hit me. I was angry.

No, more than that. I was livid. My ears burned and my internal fire broke within me. *Mark*, I thought. Why should have Mark died so young? When I was nineteen, I was just getting to know him as an adult and get to have a real relationship with him. He was the life of the party, charismatic, and had a genuinely good heart. And his life was taken so soon. But as a 19-year-old, Mark seemed so old. So wise. So full of life. I couldn't help but look up to him. And here I was, the same age and I was far from the vibrant life he was.

Instead, I was locked in a cage for trying to be in control, my addiction of choice. I controlled myself in that I only drank beer, as I knew I got sick and feisty when drinking hard alcohol. I controlled my environment to ensure my small, safe world stayed that way. I controlled the people and relationships in my life by only giving so much of myself, for fear of them learning the truth about my past. I controlled my outcomes to ensure that I would graduate college, get married, and do all of the things in the right order that I was raised to believe in. I did everything right. And yet, here I am. None of the factors that I controlled were helping me. In all reality, obsessing and controlling the outcomes made me spiral out of control and I didn't even know it.

My defeated scream was lost with the echo of my fist hitting the metal bench I was sitting on. I sobbed even harder.

Once I realized even the guards were probably used to a lot of commotion coming from the drunk tank and that they would not be coming to check on me, I started taking deeper breaths and became more aware of my environment: The putrid smell of stale urine. The small mailbox opening where they place the tray of food. I lightly grazed my shaking hand over a carving on the metal wall next to the bench. The multitude of horrific carvings and etchings in the metal made me question how the addicts who were detoxing for days carved them. I had to give all of my personal belongs over to the officers and drop it in a large manila envelope as I was admitted. The officer saw the fear in my eyes, as I was assured it was safe and that I would get my beautifully, custom designed engagement ring back when discharged.

As my eyes moved towards the industrial toilet bolted to the floor and wall, my lower abdomen rumbled. *Oh, hell no*, I thought. *No. No. No.* It was then that I bargained my only chip. *Please, God. Please let me hold it until I get out of here*, I begged. *You know I won't do this ever again. Please, don't let me pee.* What worried me most wasn't necessarily holding my pee. I had been battling a severe case of Irritable Bowel Syndrome and I was more worried that I'd shit my brains out due to gut rot in this tiny, metal box and have to sit in the stench of that for the remainder of my incarceration.

Since I handed over my watch, I didn't know what time it

was. I didn't know how long I'd been in there or when exactly they'd discharge me. I heard the officers say that Minnesota had a mandatory fourteen-hour incarceration, yet when Samantha got her DUI, she got out on bail. *How did she get out right away and I have to sit in here?*

Because you're not worth saving. Ah, there it is. The familiar voice filling my head with thoughts of unworthiness. *You're worse than she is. You need to learn where your place is. Even the officers aren't checking on you. You're not worth it. God gave you a second chance when you were fifteen. Mark's death gave you a wakeup call. And look how you lived your life. Worthless.*

Tears of regret and shame silently poured down my face. Almost a sign of defeat compared to the hot, angry tears that poured out earlier. These were different. These tears were filled with sorrow, lost love, and another life lost. Mine. I laid down on the bench and let them fall down the sides of my eyes. I could feel them move down to my ears and hear them drop down on the metal, while others made my wild hair damp. My body started shivering again from the dampness that I felt inside and out.

God, please. I'm so sorry for this pathetic life I have been leading, I prayed. *I don't know how I got here. I am so sad. All the time, I am just so sad. And I'm so angry at everyone. They don't see me. They don't truly see all of me. How hurt, how broken, how confused I am. Only you do, and here I am. Broken, again. The second chance at life you gave me, I've fucked it up yet again. Where do I go from here? How do I pretend that everything is okay after this? I'm so tired of pretending. I just want to go back to when I was a little girl again under the Mighty Oak. It didn't hurt back then. I didn't hurt. I want wide open spaces, big, expansive skies, and to not be broken. But I can't have that. I'll never have that again. I'll always be broken. Please, God. Help me heal. I don't want to be like this.*

Through my silent tears, I accepted my broken path for what it was. For the remainder of my incarceration, I silently prayed this same prayer over and over again. A prayer for peace. A prayer for healing. A prayer for my broken past and for a less broken future.

When I was released, I walked out of the same overhead door I was taken into the county jail to find Aaron waiting for me in his red dually pickup. I sat in silence as he drove me the 30 minutes back to my apartment. I didn't say a word as he filled me in on the events after my arrest, how he tried to bail me out and how they wouldn't let him.

I kept my head down in complete shame. "Are you ashamed of me?" I finally asked, breaking the silence, looking tearfully at him.

"No," he replied gently, grabbing my hand to hold. "But now you know better." It was then that I realized that he was the one who truly saw and loved me for who I was.

Broken, and all.

• • •

I tried to steady my hands as I gripped the steering wheel as I drove the 50 miles from my apartment to my parent's house. *I'm so ashamed. How could I have been so stupid?* I repeated over and over in my head. *My whole world is over.*

As I continued on the straight and narrow two-lane road, I knew the cold December night wasn't why I was shivering so bad. The radio was on; however, I couldn't even hear it with how loud the words were in my head. Repeating the shameful acts that I just encountered in the past 24 hours. *How am I supposed to explain this?* I thought. *A mistake. I made a terrible mistake. I could've killed someone. How stupid am I? I can't even stand the thought of myself right now.*

I could see the outside lights on, greeting me home. The same cedar house wrapped around by the familiar woods that I embraced as a little girl. All the same, yet now different. Or maybe it was I who was different. I took a deep breath as I wiped my tears before I got out of the car. *You've got to just say it. There's no way around it.*

I walked in the back door with my laundry, greeted by my mom in the kitchen. "Hey, Babe!" I heard as I slid my laundry across the linoleum and stood back up. Choking back tears, I turned to her and instantly, she knew.

"What's wrong?" my mom asked, searching my eyes for an answer. I darted my eyes to avoid contact before she could look too hard. In the background, I saw my dad come around the corner of the dining room into the kitchen just as I opened my mouth.

"I'm so sorry," I said. "I was arrested last night." That was all I could squeak out before I fell apart.

"Ohhhh, Kathryn. What for? Are you okay?" asked my mom. I could hear the worry in her voice, yet I could feel the shame mounting within me.

Trying to catch my breath in between sobs, I somehow mustered the rest of the words I had practiced the entire drive home out. "I got a DUI last night. I spent the night in jail and Aaron picked me up this afternoon."

She rushed over to embrace me, and I had never felt so relieved in my life to have my mom hold me. After a few moments of silence as she held me, she asked, "Did you cry the whole way here?"

I nodded as the tears continued to fall.

"Here, take off your jacket and boots and let's get you warm," she instructed. I watched as my mom busied herself with the mindless task of starting my laundry. I noticed after Mark died, it was a coping mechanism for her. Something to busy her hands while her mind raced.

After she finished, I sat down at the counter while my mom leaned up against it across from me. Clearly ready for details, she dove right in. "What happened last night? Where were you? Who were you with? Are you okay?" My dad, silent and stoic as he was, came back and stood at the end of the counter to listen. Not to offer any advice, just to be present and listen. I went into a few specifics leading up to the arrest, like where we were, who I was with, and the like, but I spared the details of anything after being pulled over. "So, what happens next?" my mom asked.

"All I know is I'll have to go to go to court and pay a fine," I said. "Anything else like how much or revoking my license is up to the judge. But I'll take care of it all." My voice cracked at the weight of that thought. I searched my mom's eyes for something, anything. Reassurance of any type, but I didn't get anything. She remained quiet and turned to finish the remaining dishes left in the sink.

"Okay," she said after letting it all sink in. "I'm sure you will."

Really? This is it? This is the end of the conversation? I thought. *No one is going to talk about the white elephant in the room about how alcoholism runs in our family? No asking if I needed treatment or help?* My mind raced. Just like that, another hard topic swept under the rug. Overwhelmed, I stood up from the counter to excuse myself. *I need space.*

I walked past my dad, choking back tears, and turned down the hall and into my childhood bedroom. The same room I found solstice for so many years, only this time was so much different. I shut the door and stood inside. I saw the new bed my parents bought after I moved out, the peaceful green color on the walls that were painted to compliment the calming purple duvet on the bed.

Only a few remnants of my childhood still remained: my play table and chairs that was covered in marker and crayon marks, stickers, and a layer of dust. A bookshelf made by a family member after my accident which held memorabilia from high school like books, pictures, and awards, along with my snow globe collection. I walked over and looked at the smiling faces, and all I saw was the same sad girl smiling back at me. Time had changed, the sadness within still remained.

I opened up the sliding closet doors to reveal more of my childhood. On the top shelf, my stuffed animal collection from when I was a little girl. Hidden in the back left corner were boxes of awards and memorabilia of accomplishments. As I held the trophy for the All-State Choral Award in my hand, nostalgia of the people I met and the places I sang at came flooding to me. A small representation of me going somewhere. At one time awards like this, they seemed so big, like I was somebody to receive them. Now as I held one in my hand, it felt like a piece of ancient history. Now I'm just a drunk with a record, I thought. I looked at the boxed of handwritten notes from Nathan and Lauren I had saved. Nathan's letterman jacket still hung among my prom dresses. I put my hand over it and felt the cool, soft leather of the sleeve, while the jingle of the many medals clanked together.

I took a step back and stared at my history sitting in that closet. For so long I had been living in the past. Out of all of my friends that I've made since I moved away, five people knew about Nathan and my accident and Mark. Five. I closed that door a long time ago, not wanting to let anyone in, yet here I was still living in that closet. Living in hopes and dreams, ignoring the pain and the betrayal, refusing to see the goodness that was right in front of me.

I sat down on the edge of my bed, facing the open closet filled with my old life. I faced it acknowledging that one foot was still in my old life while I was desperately trying to build a new life without it.

God? Mark? I need you, I pleaded. *Please, I beg of you. I don't want to live like this any longer. I am ready. I am ready to release this hold I have on the past. I need you to help me move forward. I am not like this. I have seen all the goodness you've brought into my life and I've only met you halfway with it. I haven't stood up on my own, yet. But I am ready. I am here, now, asking for you to help me. Please, show me the way. I am ready. I know I am made for more.*

After a few minutes, I lifted my head and looked at the closet. Nothing had changed, but I had. I was ready to let go. I stood up to close the closet when I caught my reflection in the mirror hanging on the wall. Even through the puffy, tear stained face and the red, swollen eyes, for the first time I saw a glimmer of hope looking back at me.

I closed the closet doors and stood hopeful that my prayer worked. Like a Phoenix, I was reborn from the ashes. Everything that I once knew was gone. My childhood home was a physical symbol of that. It was up to me to rise again. And I was determined to do that. I was not going to let my mistake and stupidity ruin anyone else's lives, emotionally or financially.

I was determined to make the next beginning one of hope and stability.

chapter eight

....

GROWING NEW LIFE

A s I left the staff meeting and sat back in my office, I couldn't help but smile. *This is it*, I thought. *I finally made it.* It had been two years since I hit rock bottom with my DUI and I felt as if I was going somewhere. I was 26, married, finished my graduate degree, and eight months pregnant with my first baby. A baby boy.

My office was small with a U-shaped desk and standard maroon business chair. Behind my computer screen, I stared at the ultrasound that I pinned on the overhead; my lone decoration. I had only been in my position for about a month, but I could tell that I was going to be happy here doing something I know and am good at. As a communications specialist in the non-profit sector, my job description included writing newsletters, appeal letters, and event planning for our small foundation to our donors. I loved every minute of it. Interviews, writing, coordinating details for events, glad-handling donors. *I was made for this*, I thought.

I rubbed my overgrown belly smiling to myself when I felt a solid kick right behind my belly button, indicating he was stretching in the little room that was left inside my huge belly. *Just make it a few more weeks, Mister.*

Ruth poked her head into my office, breaking my thoughts. "Whatchya doing for lunch? Want to head out with me and Steve?" she asked.

"Sure, I have no plans," I said. "But I have a meeting with the graphic designer at 1:00 to get this newsletter laid out." I slumped over my desk and said, "And then I have an appointment at 3:00, so I won't be back after."

"We'll leave at 11:30," Ruth said. "That'll give us plenty of time for you to get back for your meeting. Is your appointment just a regular one?"

"I'll have another ultrasound to see what my fluid levels are at, and then just monitoring," I replied. "This is ultrasound number ten. Can you believe that?"

"They're just making sure our boy is all well inside," Ruth smiled. She always referred to him as "our baby" because she knew how alone I felt having to do all of this by myself. Aaron was working long, gruesome days and I was left with my thoughts most of the time. Not a grand combination for someone who tries to fix (read: control) anything and everything to fit neatly into my box. Ruth was just as invested in this babe as I was, as I asked her every pregnancy question under the sun to prepare myself. As a mom of three already, Ruth knew exactly how hormonal I was which was layered within the worry.

The worry was thick with me, unfortunately. I had prayed for this baby for so long. I read every book I could get my hands on. I created relationships with women across the United States through message boards on *The Bump's* website. All of us who were trying to conceive moving through the trimesters, sharing concerns, milestones, and supporting each other along the way. But it wasn't lost on me that not everyone made it to 40 weeks easily...or at all.

"Just shout when you're ready to go. I'll be here. Or in the bathroom," I chided. I turned back to my computer and tried to engross myself into my work for the next few hours, but my mind kept distracting me, along with the extra kicks from the inside.

I went to our first ultrasound at 20 weeks to find out if we were having a boy or girl, but I had already known that it was a boy. My intuition was strong, and I just *knew*. I knew that God would give me a boy who wouldn't leave me; someone that I could love unconditionally and receive that love in return. Something that I so desperately needed, especially after losing two boys in my life already.

I only had a few weeks left before my firstborn son was due, but in all reality he could make his appearance known at any time. We had a rocky pregnancy, with many unknowns. The control freak in tried desperately to go with the flow of everything, but inside I was a wreck, breaking down almost every night in tears.

Each night I thanked God for letting us get through another day and prayed for a healthy baby. Our ultrasound indicated markers in his heart; a possible genetic defect and we wouldn't know the full extent of damage until he was born. Specialists, routine ultrasounds, additional genetic testing, and tossing the term of Down Syndrome became familiar in our appointment schedule.

Additionally, I was monitored three days per week for two hours at a time due to low amniotic fluid from the time I was 29 weeks. On the scale of appropriate amniotic fluid being 7-14, with an average of 12, I was sitting at a 5.2. I managed to hover around 7 for the rest of my pregnancy, but the fact that a cesarean at any moment was not out of the question ravaged me.

Little did I know that this sweet baby boy was just giving me a small taste of the emotional rollercoaster that was to come.

• • •

It was September 1, 2010. After being sent home twice, finally being induced, over 27 hours of labor, a fantastic epidural cocktail and only 15 minutes of pushing, I was relieved to hear the words, "It's a boy!" from my doctor, as she held him in the air for me to see.

I was exhausted and in total shock at what just happened. She placed him on my warm chest. *Oh my God, he's here! He's actually here*, I thought. I looked from this sweet, perfect baby boy up to Aaron who was behind my shoulder and I saw the look of pride and accomplishment in his eyes. The quiet boy that I fell in love with was speechless. After all these years, I knew what his heart was saying.

Turning back to my doctor with tears in my eyes, "Is he okay?" I cautiously asked, guarding my heart. All of the extra appointments, monitoring, and testing mounted to this moment right now. I felt it, but I needed confirmation.

"He's absolutely perfect, Kathryn. No Down Syndrome. No heart malfunctions," my doctor confirmed, smiling back to me, which silently gave me permission to finally exhale. I felt the cool tears of relief stream down my face.

"What's his name?" she asked.

I smiled at Aaron, looked down at my newest love and then looked back at her. "James," I replied.

"All good and perfect things come from above. James 1:18," my doctor recited. "Absolutely fitting for you two. I mean, three."

The next few hours after delivery were a blur of switching rooms, family rotating in and out, and getting acquainted with the new little man in my life. I soaked in every feature of James' face, although I already knew it from all the times I stared at it on the ultrasound screen. But seeing it in front of me was something totally different. The little ball at the end of his nose, just like mine. The deep blue of his eyes. The few wispy blonde hairs that stuck out underneath his newborn cap. His little puckered lips. The dimples on his hands and long fingers. He was absolutely perfect, yet I couldn't help but feel a deep sense of dread looming. *When is the other shoe going to drop?* I thought. *We are so happy. We are finally a little family. Surely it can't stay like this forever?*

I was right, it wouldn't. What I didn't realize was that it was going to turn so quickly.

Aaron slept haphazardly on the small pullout couch that was in my postpartum room but resembled more of a grown kid in a toddler bed. His 6'4" large Norwegian frame dominated the couch, and it became a running joke with the nurses during the night shifts of how his legs dangled off while he slept.

I appreciated finally being able to sleep on my stomach, but of course was awoke many times for nursing James. I was dead set on nursing and creating a strong bond with James yet was not prepared for the amount of work that it would take. I felt a societal responsibility to nurse. I was inundated by breast is best campaign, as that was the question I was asked over and over again by family, friends, and my doctor leading up to having James. I watched friends and family do so effortlessly (or so it seemed) and here I was already frustrated and confused.

"You'll get used to it," said a nurse. "It's hard. Hard for baby and hard for you. But you're trying."

In the early morning light and after hearing me grumble trying to nurse, Aaron arose from his restless sleep, checked his phone, and stated, "Well, I'm heading out."

Taken aback, I sat up and looked at him. "Uh, excuse me? Where are you going?" I asked, bewildered where he could possibly be going this early in the morning and after becoming a family of three.

"Work," he replied nonchalantly. "I had 13 missed calls yesterday. Apparently nothing can get done while I'm gone." As shop foreman, we had come to learn that any and all problems were Aaron's problem.

"What about us?" I asked wide-eyed, still holding a sleepy James in my arms. I was not ready to do this alone.

"I'll be back tonight," he said. "You'll have a lot of visitors and I don't need to be here."

Shocked and hormonal, looking down at our newborn, I squeezed my eyes closed trying to hold back tears. *Don't leave me now, Mister. Please, just stay*, I silently begged. *Please see me. Please see us. Don't go. I need you.*

And just like that, I felt Aaron kiss me on the top of my head and James on the forehead before walking out the door.

All alone. That's how I do life, I thought as the heavy door latched. *Everyone leaves me all alone.*

• • •

Aaron was right, I did have a steady stream of family and friends that came up to visit and meet James. I told and retold his birth story and in between visitors, I agonized at trying to force a bond with us nursing.

"Why is this so hard?" I cried to my nurse who had her hands on my breast and James, trying to get a good latch. "Who ever said this is natural?"

"It takes time, Kathryn," my nurse tried to comfort me. "They say five weeks is the magic number for you two to finally feel like you've got this down."

"Five weeks?" I cried out, bewildered. "I can't even do this, and it's been a day. How the hell am I supposed to do this for five weeks?" I was already defeated, nursing for an hour at a time just to do it again in two.

"You can do it," she reassured me. "You'll find a groove that works for you." Although I already knew deep down that this may be the death of our bond, versus creating it. Once we finished, my nurse left me and James to ourselves. I got up to look out at the dreary September sky, noticing the mist had not lifted since I was admitted two days earlier.

I sat down in the rocking chair and stared at James perfectly content swaddled in my arms. Yet something felt off. It was 7 p.m., visiting hours were over and Aaron wasn't back yet. *Welcome to our new normal, kid*, I sighed, heavy hearted. *I'm sorry that this is what you get. Me.*

The tears flowed effortlessly. "I'm so sorry," I sobbed, rocking James in my arms. "I'm sorry that I can't give you the family you deserve." There was the shame that I knew so well, creeping up and out like the demon it was. "You deserve so much more than what I can give you. You need a mommy and a daddy." The thought of the perfect family of three was already shattered by James' second day on earth. I knew that Aaron worked hard to provide for our family, but I thought maybe, just maybe, that James would be the link that would make our bond stronger than ever. And he did, just not the way I had visualized for the past 10 months.

In the days and months after James' birth, my shame and anger turned into a whole new level. Nursing became a crux between us, where I resented him for not latching and exclusively pumping became my arch nemesis. I resented Aaron for leaving me alone with a baby when I didn't know how to handle one. I finally felt a reprieve when I could take James to daycare at six weeks old and somewhat breathe for a few hours to myself. By the time I went back to work, James had reached a colicky stage, I was exhausted beyond belief, and Aaron was back to working an average of 72 hours each week and coming home by 9 p.m. on a good day. My resentment towards him increased and came out towards James. I was spiraling down and looking for a way out. The demons of postpartum depression had a strong grip on me.

One night when James was in his bewitching hours of crying straight from 5 p.m. to 8 p.m., which was a nightly routine, I cried right along with him. I had given up and I had nowhere to go. The walls of our small two-bedroom apartment felt like they were closing in, and I called Aaron out of sheer desperation.

"Are you coming home yet?" I exasperatedly asked over the wailing of James in the background.

"I'll be leaving shortly," Aaron replied.

"No. No, that's not soon enough," I said in between tears trying to catch my breath. "I can't do this!"

"Just hang on. I'll be there soon," he reassured me. Only, he didn't get it. I was already past gone. I hung up the phone and prayed that I could make it the next hour until Aaron got home. I tried not to let that black hole consume me. Once I heard the deadbolt unlock, I stood up and was at the door as Aaron walked in. My tearstained face and exhausted demeanor gave it all away. Aaron held out his arms and I felt the sweet release of letting James go. Both of us who were wailing for the past few hours were now comforted by Aaron's presence. We needed his calm demeanor and he filled the massive void that we both felt.

"How do you do that?" I asked defeated.

"What?" Aaron replied, his calm, collected self. Nothing ever rattled him.

"Complete us," I said. "You walk in and James just knows. Once he stops crying, I can stop and can finally breathe again. It's always you."

Aaron just shrugged and walked over to the couch to lay down with James on his chest, finally finding sleep.

• • •

Months later, I look back down at the pregnancy test with tears in my eyes. "I can't be pregnant. I already have a baby," acknowledging a sleeping James, only nine months old, in the other room. I stared at the two pink lines on the pregnancy test and then look up at Aaron with tears in my eyes.

"It's good," Aaron reassured me.

The all too familiar feeling of shame overwhelmed me. "No." I looked at Aaron. "Mister, I can't," I said. "I didn't ask for this." *This is not a part of the plan*, I thought. *We're just getting our footing. This can't happen.*

"It'll be okay," he said, trying to sound optimistic, pulling me in closer. "We make cute kids, at least."

"Stop! That doesn't help," I said. "I'm finally getting the hang of this. I'm just now getting back into my life," I confessed to Aaron, with my head still down. "I can't have two babies."

"We'll figure it out," he said. "We always do."

My mind went into hyper-drive. *Two babies. Two. How am I to raise two babies? How are we going to afford this?* My heart ached. People who were trying so hard to have babies couldn't and here I was, upset that God gave me another? *How ungrateful could I be? I must be some sort of derived person*, I thought.

• • •

It was just in those past couple months that James and I finally found the bond we both desperately needed. I stopped obsessing about nursing or exclusively pumping and relaxed into the notion that he could not only survive but thrive on formula. The level of added stress I placed upon myself was ridiculous. I completely judged myself for not meeting my own sky-high expectations, falling flat on my face more than once in the motherhood journey. Additionally, once I got back into the groove of work, I started finding myself again, knowing that I was good at what I did. I had just finished hosting a huge golf tournament that raised over $70,000 for the local cancer center and I was over the moon. Plus, Aaron and I finally worked on our communication of what kind of support James and I need versus what we were getting. But the biggest change was that I moved past the idea of what I thought life should look like versus enjoying how my life was unfolding. Just because we don't have the white picket fence doesn't mean what we do have isn't beautiful.

"Kathryn, quit comparing us to everyone else," Aaron reassured me as I broke down yet again from one of my hormonal fits. "Just because it's on Facebook doesn't mean it's the truth. You know they don't have it all together! Nobody does!"

Through the tears, I knew my heart knew. An acquaintance I knew was living through a tragedy with her 5-month-old baby. Thanks to social media, I read that he was found unresponsive at his daycare, was life-flighted to the nearest children's hospital and in critical condition and was fighting for his very fragile life. It was that moment that everything hit home. I grabbed a sleeping 9-month-old James from his crib and perched him on my already budding belly and rocked him in his room. Silent tears and silent prayers washed over me and him as the hours passed. I couldn't allow myself to let him go.

"I'm sorry that I can't give you new cars or family vacations or a house," I said. "I'm sorry I can't even give you a daddy who is home for supper. But I can give you a fierce faith. I can give you unconditional love. I can give you more strength, more courage, and more determination to become the best person you can be. Your daddy is a great example of that. I promise you I will give you everything you need, even if there is a new little love coming into our lives."

And with that, I continued to pray for his safety, for his strength, for his health, and for his heart. For James had already taught me so much already, I was determined to give that much and more back to him.

• • •

Two weeks later, still in shock that I was pregnant, we visit my parents for the fourth of July. The sun was beating down and my mom and I were out on the front porch having coffee watching James play by our feet with the same toys I played with as a kid.

I had already prayed long and hard at how and when I was going to break the news. To be completely honest, I didn't want to. I was so worried, as my mom wasn't great with surprise announcements. When I called to say I was engaged, her response was in a sarcastic offended tone, "Well, Aaron didn't ask us for permission." Or when I broke the news about being pregnant with James, she sat down in shock and said, "Oh wow, I have to sit for a moment. I can't believe my baby is going to have a baby."

Knowing that my mom wasn't one to beat around the bush I just dove in. "Mom, I don't know how to say this, so I'm just gonna say it," I confessed, keeping my tearful eyes on James, filled with shame at what I was about to say. "I'm pregnant."

There was a long pause, which felt like an eternity before my mom broke the silence. The same anxiety that creeped up whenever I had to tell her something big creeped in awaiting her response.

"Well...aren't you going to be busy," she said.

Just like that, the wind was knocked out of me. *Seriously?*

That's what you're going to say to me? Don't you see that I'm scared? Don't you see me holding back the tears? Don't you see me at all?

Not finding the compassion or support that I needed, I continued, "Well, I'm just saying that I'm not fully prepared for this and having two babies under two is going to be hard..." I trailed off.

"You'll make it work," she replied. My heart was shattered. Nobody, not even my mom saw how scared and broken I felt on the inside.

Later on, I confessed how this interaction with my mom went with my coworker Ruth, and she responded to me, "There's a reason why you're pregnant for ten months, because sometimes it takes all ten months to fully accept a new little love in your life." Holy hell, was that true. Just when I thought I had finally gotten a handle on my postpartum depression, my newly enraged hormones lit that fire back up. *The shame and guilt that I had for bringing another child into the world when I didn't feel ready. That I couldn't handle two babies. That my best friend just lost another baby to miscarriage and there I was ungrateful to be pregnant in the first place was unreal.*

I cried myself to sleep for four months straight. After the heartbreaking reaction from my mom of having another baby, I didn't even announce to anyone that I was pregnant until after twenty weeks when I knew I was having another boy. Another boy who would fill a void I didn't know I had. Another boy who stretched me and saved me. Another boy who multiplied my love and my lap and demonstrated my ability to manage an organized chaos that my life soon turned into.

My Drewbear.

Living up to his grandeur ways, coming in like a bull on his exact due date of February 29, 2012—Leap Year Day. Drew showed me what it was like to have an unbreakable bond from the beginning; a complete 180-degree turn from the bonding experience I had with James. This time it was peaceful, more whole. Of course, due to societal pressure, I was determined to try nursing again, but the moment I came home from the hospital and saw the breast pump on the kitchen table, I felt what was probably resembled Post Traumatic Stress Disorder. Drew took his first bottle like a champ.

Drew showed me what sleeping through the night was at seven weeks old. He showed me that no matter what our family looked like, you know, loud and full and untraditional with Aaron gone all the time, that we were all in this together and full of love. He showed me that I was, in fact, more than capable of handling two boys under the age of two. Like a goddamn pro, actually. I wasn't a bad mom like I shamed myself for being. I was, in fact, a great mom. I just had to learn that the hard way.

With James, I was too busy trying to survive on schedules and sore nipples and some crazy idea of how motherhood was supposed to look like instead for what it was. With Drew, I appreciated the little moments like coos, his first giggles, needing to be near James at all times, and watching how James took on the big brother role like the natural leader he was.

• • •

One afternoon, I wheeled the stroller out our back door and I held it open for a toddling James to follow, holding his baggie of animal crackers. We didn't make it far, just enough to sneak in the last of the afternoon sun as we set up our picnic on the small patch of grass behind our apartment building. After a long day at work and missing my boys, I tried hard to get outside for even just 20 minutes each day to enjoy some sunshine and giggles to help with my depression. Aaron still never made it home before bedtime, so even if it was 20 minutes of just being present with these boys before the long night, I found that made a huge difference in my energy.

I laid out the blanket, unpacked our PB&J sandwiches, two apple sauce pouches, more animal crackers, a water bottle, a sippy cup, a bottle, a few cars, and a beach ball. As Drew sat in my lap, we watched as James chased that beach ball in the sun and screamed and laughed with sheer joy. Every two minutes or so, James would run back over to the blanket, take a bite of his sandwich and eat a few crackers before he'd run off again.

"Doo! Watch!" he'd yell from a few yards away. "Doo! Mommy! Yook!" before he'd try to kick the ball haphazardly again while laughing at himself. I smiled as I soaked in the sun on my face and leaned in to kiss the top of Drew's face. *Ages two years and six months are good*, I thought. *No, not just good.* James squealed again which made Drew belly laugh back at him. *We're happy.* I breathe in their giggles and acknowledge my sense of self and newfound confidence in my mothering abilities that are finally cracking through.

Lesson learned.

The Universe knew exactly what I needed at exactly the right time. God knew that I needed these boys to learn how to be present and exhale again. To trust in His timing and not my own. To learn that there is no such thing as a normal family, and to be okay with the imperfect one I had in front of me. But most of all, I learned to trust that the other shoe doesn't always drop.

Because of Drew, he taught me to find joy in the journey.

chapter nine

FALLING AWAY

As I stood manning our resource table inside the Memorial Union on the university's campus, I felt the familiar buzz of my phone in my pocket of someone calling me. I quickly glance down to see if it was Ruth, my former coworker, calling to tell me something unexpectedly came up and she couldn't make our standing Thursday lunch date. Instead I was shocked to see my brother Matt's name appear on the screen. *Why in the world is he calling*, I silently ask myself. *He never calls. What could be so important?* I picked up.

"Did Dad call you?" he asked before I had even had the chance to answer the phone. Even more bewildered as to why my brother who lived in Indiana would be asking about my dad calling, who lived just an hour from me in Minnesota.

"Nope. What's up?" thinking this is the most ridiculous conversation to be having in the middle of the day.

"Mom's been taken by ambulance to the hospital in Grand Forks," Matt started to say. "Dad should be on his way."

"Wait...what?" I said. "What's going on?"

"Mom...she had a stroke," Matt blurted out, followed by silence.

A stroke? I thought. *No, that's not possible.*

"How do you know this?" I asked, still questioning how he knows what's going on in Indiana and I'm still in the dark.

"Timmy O. called," Matt replied. "He was one of the paramedics who responded, and he called me when he couldn't get ahold of Dad." *Timmy O. Of course*, I thought. A beloved soul who is intertwined so much into our lives as a best friend to both of my brothers, our second cousin, and a groomsman in my wedding. "I got ahold of Dad and he is on his way to the hospital."

"Okay," I respond, unable to say anything else as the words *a stroke* repeated in my mind over and over.

"Okay," Matt repeated, unsure what else to say. "So, you'll go there?"

"Yes." I said, starting to shake.

As parents and students billowed in and out of the Memorial Union around me, I stood there staring at the blank screen on my phone in my trembling hand. I then dialed Ruth's number. Ruth picked me up on Mondays and Thursdays, our regular lunch days for the past three years. It has been almost a year since I left the Foundation and working with Ruth every day, yet we remained very close friends.

"Hey, I'm just crossing over the bridge," she said instead of answering her usual hello.

"I can't do lunch," I said. "My brother Matt just called. My mom," my voice broke. "She had a stroke."

"Where are you?" Ruth demanded.

"At the Union," I responded, tears started swelling in my

eyes. As a success coach in career services, I provided support to students figuring out what they wanted to be when they grow up. I often found myself watching these students grow before my eyes just as their parents do; giving them the foundation to go out in the world and do great things. Now I see these parents doting on and sharing in the excitement of their child's next new adventure during Freshman Orientation while I received the news that my mom may never do that for me again. Hell, in my fierce independence growing up, I never let her dote on me anyway. *But that doesn't mean I didn't appreciate her trying. The sweet juxtaposition of a parent hanging onto their baby and yet wanting to let them fly,* I thought as I squeezed my eyes shut.

"I'm at the stoplight, waiting to turn. Wait right there. I will get you," Ruth said calmly to me, as I forgot that she was still on the line.

"Okay," I said, hanging up. As a temporary employee with no benefits, I took my dream job only eight months ago on a wing and a prayer hoping it would turn into a full-time position. I had felt so complacent in my old job writing newsletters, doing the same thing day in and out, not feeling challenged. Stagnant. But there? I felt a sense of ease being back working for my alma mater assisting students, utilizing so many of my skills and abilities, not to mention degrees.

When I saw Ruth's gray Toyota Avalon pulling up the curved drive, I walked out to have the sweltering heat hit my face. It was Thursday, July 18, 2013 and we had been experiencing a super-hot and humid summer already, with temps reaching mid-80s, which is fairly uncommon this early in the summer in the Upper Midwest.

I weaved through more students and parents enjoying the sunshine as they walked to their cars parked out front. As I climbed into her car, Ruth took off for the hospital, only a half mile from campus. "What do you know?" she asked. I repeated my entire conversation with Matt to her, which was not much.

"A stroke," I repeated quietly as we drove over the overpass. With horror in my eyes, I turned to Ruth as the severity of what a stroke could possibly mean. "What if she can't walk or talk again? There's a gal from Fertile, someone who graduated with Matt, his mom. She had a stroke years ago and even after therapy, she can hardly talk and walks with a cane. Oh my God. What if that's my mom?" I asked tearfully. Time and traffic suddenly felt still. *What if I never hear her say my name again? What if she never gets to read to my boys again? Who will have Thanksgiving?* My biggest fears were compounding. *She's the glue that holds everyone together, everyone knows that.*

"Let's wait to get answers first," Ruth said calmly. "Is your dad meeting you at the emergency room?"

"I assume so? He doesn't have a cell to call," I replied, silently cursing his old farmer habits and not ever getting a cell phone.

"Of course, he lives on the farm. Why would he need a cell?" Ruth agreed sarcastically, trying to cut the tension as she pulled up to the ER door. "I will wait for you as long as you need. I'll park the car and will sit in the waiting room in case you need me."

"Okay," I said, looking at her with immense gratitude knowing that I needed a maternal support during the next unknown. "Thank you."

• • •

In the hospital, I ran down the hallway the nurse pointed me down and turned the corner to her room only be stopped dead in my tracks at the sight of my mom. *Oh my God*, I thought. There she was, flat on a gurney, motionless and fully intubated. My worst fears were confirmed. The look on my face must have given away that I was a loved one, because the doctor on call swooped in and blocked my view of her.

"Are you Gay's daughter?" he asked

"Yes," I said, trying to focus on his face and shake the image of my mom out of my head.

"I'm Dr. Anu, the physician on call when your mom came in this morning," he proceeded, and started escorting me out the door. "Let's go to the family room and wait for your dad."

"Is he coming?" I asked.

"The paramedics who brought your mom in said he is on his way," Dr. Anu responded.

We made our way back down the hall and turned another corner, practically running into my dad. Dr. Anu introduced himself the same way he did to me, only shaking my dad's hand. He then opened the door to a dimly lit, small room with an old couch, two chairs, a table with old magazines and a TV with HGTV on mute. I sat down on the couch, my dad continued to stand, hands shoved in his front pockets. I see he just came in from the farm, his work boots still on, but he changed his shirt into one of his clean, short sleeved flannels.

"We have Gay stabilized at this moment, but we are doing many tests to see what is going on inside that brain of hers," Dr. Anu started. "Do either of you know of any medical history of hers? Any medications or hospitalizations that Gay has had in recent years?"

My dad and I looked at each other, bewildered. "No, not at all," my dad said.

"She just ran the Fargo Marathon in May," I said, reiterating that this must be some mistake. "She was as healthy as a horse."

"Okay. Well, we did a CT scan, and something showed up,"

Dr. Anu said. Making eye contact with both my dad and I, Dr. Anu continued. "What we do know is that she had multiple seizures this morning. Meaning, the something we found on her brain triggered those seizures and we're doing all we can to get to the bottom of things right now."

I looked at how pale my dad looked, even in such a dark room. He now was leaning against the chair for support; bracing to what was to come next. I watched as Dr. Anu had one leg up and was half-sitting, half-standing on the table across the room from us, while my dad and I felt the weight of the world being cast upon us from the opposite side.

"Her scans are up in neurology right now, and they're giving it a good look through to help us see what we're dealing with," Dr. Anu proceeded on. "We think it's one of two things. The best-case scenario is that this is an old bleed that crystalized and that's what triggered the seizures. If that's the case, we can take a swift action to clear up the bleed and continue to watch for any other aneurism activity moving forward. Worst case scenario is that the spot on her brain is a tumor," Dr. Anu stated. "We don't know if that's what we're dealing with, but if it is, surgery and a follow up with the Cancer Center will be the next steps."

I felt the wind being sucked out of my chest as he spoke. "So, it's not a stroke?" I asked for clarification, as that's what Matt told me.

"No, there is no sign of an actual stroke," Dr. Anu confirmed. "We don't know exactly what it is yet, but we are optimistic that we will get to the bottom of this and have a plan shortly."

"What's next?" my dad asked, ever so quietly. I looked over at him. *Is it possible that he is shrinking in front of me? I ask myself. Why is it that people shrink when faced with something so big or is the problem so big that people physically cower towards it?*

"Gay will be admitted to ICU. There they will try to wake her up,

134

as she is heavily sedated right now. An induced coma, actually," Dr. Anu responded. "We needed to make her brain quit having so much activity to stop any seizures, so the next step is to wait and see."

A wave of reality hit me, and I asked, "Wait, did the seizures do any damage?" Dr. Anu was quiet for a moment, thinking about his response before he answered. "We don't know," he said. "We won't know any extend of damage until she wakes up, so it's imperative that we do all we can to wake her up slowly and see what we're dealing with."

My mind raced. *They don't know anything.*

And then the unthinkable thought hit me. "Will she wake up?"

"Again, we won't know anything until we start weaning her off the meds and see how she responds and what we're dealing with," Dr. Anu answered gently. "Right now, we need to give her brain a rest and wait for Neurology to come back with more reports. A page came through on his beeper, breaking the painful silence we were all sitting in. "Excuse me," he said as he left. He paused in the doorway and he told us that someone will come and escort us to the ICU when she has been transferred.

I looked back over at my dad again, only this time his back was against me as he faced the ugly flowered wallpaper. The energy in that little room was eerie and intense, as I suspect it is most days when families get horrific news about their loved ones. Overtones and shadows of death, diagnoses, grim outlooks, and percentages of survival. I can't imagine anyone needing to be escorted to this little room for good news. Nothing about this room was bright and cheery; it screamed doom and gloom.

"We need it to be a brain bleed," I said with forced optimism. I needed something to focus on. Any glimmer of hope. My dad, instead, stayed silent, staring at the wall.

135

• • •

By the sheer determination of my mother and God's grace (and I'm sure with Mark's help) my mom came out of her induced coma, slowly and steadily. It was Saturday morning, only two days after she was admitted; yet it felt like it had been an eternity since Thursday at noon. It was a long two days of weaning of medications and watching her go from helpless and motionless to stubbornly trying to get tubes and IVs out was absolutely heartbreaking on so many levels. Scared for her and for myself. I was not prepared to mother my own mother. A paradox I didn't want to be a part of. I was still the baby of this family, and yet there I was, in charge.

A running list of all the other things I was in charge of or accomplished washed over me. *None of that matters right now*, I thought. *Washing Drew's cloth diapers, reminding Aaron of James' baby well visit next week, running to Target to pick up a present for my niece's birthday, writing a recommendation letter for a student, remodeling our fixer upper house, the extra committees I asked to join at work...I took on all those things. And yet, what for? On the outside, everything looks picture perfect. I've done everything right; in the right order. And for what? None of it matters. My mom is fighting for her life and all these miniscule things pale in comparison as I'm the one signing papers, conferring with doctors and nurses, prepping for the next stages, all while keeping everyone up to date. Everything to everyone, yet again.*

I remained steadfast by my mom's side and used the moments where friends and family visited to take a break in the waiting room outside of the ICU, but this morning was different. I just needed to get out of that sterile environment as I didn't think I could handle anymore buzzing from all the charting, beeping, and blood pressure cuffs automatically running in the background. Renée, my second mom and dear friend, had just left that morning after staying by my side for two days. I was relieved to finally have peace to breathe yet was haunted at going through this alone.

My thoughts immediately went to my boys and Aaron, who swooped in to take care of everything at home, so I could be here. With the boys at ages 1 and 2, it was a coordinated chaos in our lives. *I so wish I had that chaos as a distraction right now, I thought. Of all the hard days and nights and that stupid wallpaper that I decided to rip down the day before the seizure, I'd take that over sitting in here any day.*

• • •

The night before, Aaron was able to sneak away while his sister watched the boys to wish me a happy anniversary. Five years married, thirteen years together, and now three tragedies. *He sure knows how to pick 'em*, I thought. *Date the girl in the back brace who already lived through hell. It can't go downhill from there. Yeah, right.*

Aaron never thought of it that way, though. He waited outside the ICU until I came out and handed me a small bouquet of flowers. I smiled as my eyes welled with tears, "I can't bring those into the ICU."

"I know," he confirmed quietly. "I'll bring them back home, but I just knew you needed them," he said as he wrapped his big arms around me the way he always did. As a teen, I remember always thinking that we perfect together because when standing, I fit right under his chin. As we hugged, I would get buried in his chest, always finding solstice in his heartbeat and drawing in a deep inhale of him. My favorite place of comfort.

We embraced for what felt like ten minutes in that bare waiting room at the end of the hall. Tears streamed down my face as I was finally able to release, trusting he would always be right there to pick me back up. When I was ready, I let go and motioned to sit in the empty chairs that surrounded us.

"What do you know?" Aaron asked quietly, still holding my hand.

"Not much," I said. "We're still waiting to hear from the doctor about what it is. She did wake up and seem somewhat lucid this afternoon, which is progress, but the nurse warned us it was still not her. She nodded in response and squeezed my hand, and about two minutes later, she drifted back off to sleep."

"But that's good," he urged, hopeful. "You think she knew it was you?"

"I think so," I said. "I mean, her nurse said she does and that's why she squeezed my hand. He told her to squeeze my hand if she has heard my voice. I've been talking to her and reading her the paper and her friends have come in to chat with her, so I know she's in there somewhere..." My voice trailed off.

"She's still there, Kathryn," he said softly. "She's stronger than you know."

• • •

I smiled to myself as I thought of Aaron and his unwavering support for me. Thinking about all that I left behind to be here, I knew that Aaron could handle anything and everything on the home front. Plus, I basically told work that I'd be back when I knew more of a timeline and what we were dealing with. It was still touch and go, so I wasn't sure what else to tell them. The male nurse who was tending to my mom for the next three days peeked his head into the waiting room where I was, and the sight of him broke my thoughts. I immediately I stood up, thinking the worst.

"Dr. Anu is here. He wants to see you," he said.

"Of course," I said, hurrying behind him to meet the doctor. The sight of Dr. Anu's handsome, dark face was contrasted by the doctor standing next to him with white blonde hair and bright blue eyes that were rimmed with circle tortoise glasses.

"Hello, again," said Dr. Anu. "I'd like for you to meet Dr. Oxenhandler, a neurosurgeon. Is your dad here?"

"No, he doesn't get here until about 11:00 am," I replied. The life of a farmer doesn't cease for illness and diagnoses, so reluctantly, my dad had to make sure the chores were done twice a day, still. Add in the hour drive to the hospital, and it made for a small window of the day that he was able to remain bedside.

Not missing a beat, Dr. Anu dove right in. "Well, we have taken a long and steady look at all of your mom's scans, the CT, MRI, and now the EKG that was taken yesterday," he started, not breaking eye contact with me. "Unfortunately, it's not what we hoped. The spot on Gay's brain is a tumor."

No, no, no. No, it's not. My stomach dropped, and I felt a lump welling in my throat.

"It looks like a slow growing tumor, it has probably been there for five to ten years, and it finally got big enough to trigger the seizures," Dr. Anu continued. "Based on all the scans and conferring with Dr. Oxenhandler, we recommend a full craniotomy to remove the tumor."

"A tumor?" I whispered softly, suddenly losing my voice and the feeling in my legs. I held onto the doorframe of my mom's ICU unit for stability.

"Surgery is scheduled for Monday, probably in the afternoon as Gay is third on the list," Dr. Oxenhandler chimed in. "We will remove the tumor and send it for a biopsy to determine what kind and grade of tumor it is. Based on the location of it and it being a primary tumor, meaning its growing from the inside of the brain, out, unfortunately they're most likely to be malignant."

"Cancer?" I squeaked out.

"Most likely, yes. Is Gay awake now?" he asked looking over my shoulder, as if the news he just delivered wasn't life changing.

"I just looked in on her before you got here. She is still quite groggy," Dr. Anu confirmed to his colleague. "She's not lucid enough to comprehend what's going on, yet."

"How about this?" asked Dr. Oxenhandler. "Why don't I come back tonight when she's more awake and your dad is here and talk to all of you together? I'll tell Gay the news and what the plan is," he said. "That way it'll give her more time to get her senses about her, and then she can ask any questions she may have."

"Okay," I replied, in complete shock, still holding myself up. I thanked the doctors and watched them walk out of the room, configuring a few more details for the next two days before surgery.

I looked over at my mom who was still resting peacefully, unable to comprehend the brevity of what was happening. She looked so peaceful and much more like herself now that the breathing tube was out. By God's sheer will, she came out of her medical induced coma last night and could speak, although at a whisper. She also recognized us and spoke our names, which made my heart sing. The seizures did not do permanent damage, but that tumor was another story.

No. I am the baby, I think to myself. *Since when did the baby of the family become the one who has to hold this? A brain tumor. Surgery. Cancer.* I manage to make my legs work far enough to get back to my uncomfortable barely-cushioned turquoise chair that I slept in the past two nights. Just when I thought we were passing a corner with my mom waking up and talking, the bomb drops. On me.

Time stood still the rest of the morning. Not sure what to think or what questions to ask or even how to process this information, I felt like I was standing on a landmine, waiting for it to explode.

Brain surgery. What does this even mean? Cancer. Chemo. Will she lose her hair? What if she dies? My thoughts bounced from fear to unwavering support back to the what ifs. *Where is everyone? Why is it so quiet all of a sudden? Why is the only thing I hear is the pounding of my heart in my chest?*

The sight of my dad walking in through the door broke my train of thoughts. The nurse was taking my mom's vitals and she was in and out of consciousness from weaning off all the meds they had pumped her petite body with. Somewhat conscious, she managed to smile as my dad walked in acknowledging his presence, but her eyes soon shut as she drifted back off to sleep.

"Did the doctor come in?" my dad turned to me and asked, not missing a beat. I was still standing on that landmine, not sure how to sidestep off without detonating a total blow.

"Yes," I replied, drawing out my answer and looking past him at the nurse hoping he would notice I needed him as a buffer. Not getting my subtle cue, the nurse got up from the computer after charting and walked out to his next patient. Fully realizing that it was going to be devastating news no matter what, I clicked into my "fixer" mode. The one that I resorted to whenever I had to step up and lead, especially when chaos ensued. *I take broken pieces and create*, I thought. *Time to pick up the pieces of what's left.* My dad was still staring at me, waiting for the update.

"Dr. Anu came in with a neurosurgeon, Dr. Oxenhandler," I started, starting to see the expression change on my dad's face. "It's not what we were hoping for. The spot on mom's head is a tumor...most likely cancerous. They've already scheduled a full craniotomy for Monday."

No words, time, or distance could surmount the vast valley that stood between my dad and I in that little room. I searched his face for something, anything. Anything that would have him understand the enormity of what I had been holding onto for the past few hours, but none of that registered. Instead I watched the horror and pain wash over him as he realized what we were facing. *A tumor. Surgery. Cancer.*

He walked over and sat down next to my mom, held her hand, and wept. The love of his life laying so peacefully and the rest of us broken inside, processing what all of this meant. Seeing him slumped over her bed, it was not lost on me that this was only the second time I have ever witnessed him crying. So vulnerable and raw, again, he looked so fragile and broken instead of being the unyielding and stoic farmer I knew him as.

"Have you called Matt?" my dad finally asked looking up at me, breaking the silence.

"No," I replied, a bit taken aback. "Am I supposed to?"

He composed himself before responding. "You better," he said, again not realizing the immense pressure that put on me. Nobody likes to be the bearer of bad news, but I found it an oxymoron that as the baby of the family, once again I stepped into the adult role and had to take action. Matt was still in Indiana, not able to drop everything with a young family and being on-call as a train engineer.

With an enormous lump in my throat and again feeling like the ultimate bearer of bad news, I grabbed my phone and walked out to the waiting room to deliver the news over and over again. First to Matt and then to the three contacts that became my speakers to the outside world; my mom's sister, Renée, and Aaron. Once the baby, now the glue that was holding this family together.

A thought ran through my mind: *God doesn't call the qualified. He calls those who are willing to lead.*

• • •

An 11mm brain tumor. That's what was removed from my mom's brain, quite successfully. There was a tiny bit under the folds of my mom's brain that Dr. Oxenhandler didn't want to get, as it was touching her motor and speech receptors in her brain, so he recommended that chemo and radiation to be the next step.

They biopsied the mass and the confirmation came back. Oligodendroglioma. *Cancer.*

It was now August, and my mom is just finishing up her fifth week of radiation treatment. She has doctor's orders not to drive for six months, so volunteers of our small community set up a carpool for the two-hour round trip to the Cancer Center, which was five days a week for the past five weeks.

I settled back in to work at the university, finally feeling like I was getting back into life. I was working extra hours each day and coming in on weekends to recoup some of the hours I missed in the week I stayed with my mom in the hospital. The guilt I carried for missing so much time as a new employee, working for less than a year and just dropping everything for my mom was profound. Feeling as if I dropped the ball on all accounts weighed heavily on me. I prided myself on being the selfless, accountable employee, as my work ethic was a high priority. To have left so unexpectedly and have others juggle my balls in the air for me felt so irresponsible and guilt-stricken. I had to make that up to everyone, ten-fold.

Yet there was a silver lining through the weight of it all. I was able to witness the strength and determination that my mom had throughout the whole ordeal has been nothing short of amazing. Miracles of strength that was undoubtedly orchestrated by Mark in heaven. Not once did I see my mom break down. Defying the odds, in just three days after her surgery, she was released with only one prescription...for an anti-seizure medication. Zero pain killers.

"Healthy as a horse," Dr. Oxenhandler described her as he

looked over all of the new scans, tests, and notes in her chart from Occupational Therapy, Physical Therapy, and Speech, Language, and Pathology. The same description I used when she was admitted.

But now the new normal began for our family. A year of chemotherapy in pill form, highly regulated as an independent Mayo Clinic study. No driving. Sick days. Chemo brain. No hair. Well, the little hair that was left after I shaved it before her craniotomy.

I tried so hard to be delicate, I thought. Right before they wheeled her down to the OR, the surgeon's assistant came up to shave three spots where they would be making the incisions. I asked if I could do it. *I didn't trust them*, I thought. *This is my mom, I'm the one who has done her hair for the past 10 years. I am going to be the one who shaves it.* As I held onto the electric shaver, I knelt on the bed behind my mom's frail body and my hand shook right along with the buzzer.

It was such an odd juxtaposition to be in. So nurturing, yet so primal. My mom, the classy, always put together and graceful woman getting her head shaved. And yet, the delicate caress and touch I used in order to give her all the grace and dignity I could. Not knowing what the outcome of this surgery was or if I'd ever get to hold onto a moment like this again, I soaked in every feature of her that I could.

As her short, soft, brown hair fell over my hands and onto the hard hospital bed by my knees, I joked, "Scars and shaved heads, mom. You're turning into a real badass." It was the only thing I could do to hold back the tears. Mom managed to laugh out loud to that thought.

And then there was my new normal. The delicate dance of balancing mothering my own babies while mothering my own mother. Needing to be in two places at once. Giving more of myself without taking the time to refill myself. Proving my worth at work to help my odds at landing a full-time job. A full-time mama to my boys. A decent wife to Aaron, who was still working ungodly hours each week. Getting back to the half-renovated bathroom that I left in pieces while I sat with my mom in the hospital.

• • •

The night I came home when my mom was released from the hospital, it was only about 8 p.m., but everyone was already in bed. The sweet relief I felt as I walked into the house washed over me. The immense joy of being in my own home, to sleep in my own bed, and to finally take a shower after seven days.

I walked down the hall and stopped to turn on the light in the bathroom and was taken aback at the sight. The streaks of wallpaper that still remained on the walls; 1979 cream paper that yellowed something awful with tiny pink hearts that resembled polka dots when standing back. Little boys' clothes on the tiled green floor from the baths that were taken a few hours prior. Toothpaste lined the avocado green sink, which hadn't been cleaned since before I left. Standing in the doorway, emotions flooded back as I grieved the life that I once knew. How the world kept turning while mine completely shattered.

"Oh for fuck's sake," I muttered. "This is my life." Tears poured down my face. I shut the door in order not to wake anyone and finally let everything out. I held onto the vanity and looked at the person who was in the mirror. For someone being just 29 years old, I hardly recognized her anymore. Everything that I had tried to become, who I tried to be, it didn't matter. I wasn't that girl anymore.

I looked back at the wall and traced my hand over the half-ripped paper that still remained. *This is my life*, I thought again. *Torn. Broken. Half here, half gone. The old me hanging on for dear life while everything is being stripped away.*

All in all, it took over 17 hours total to get that damn wallpaper off, broken up over the span of a seven days. I used every method hoping for a quick fix: scouring, steaming, soaking in laundry detergent. Yet, to no prevail. Just like the deep transformation that was going on inside of me, there was not going to be a quick fix. Just a lot of long nights, tears of frustration, sorrow, and hope, but most of all, keeping at it. Working through the pain, trusting the outcome will be worth the heartache. I took breaks when overwhelmed, yet the determination to get that damn bathroom done was strong. I had to push through. It was the only thing I knew how to do.

Keep moving forward to a new normal.

An oddly familiar place, as I'd done this twice before. To learn how to live with an open, empty hole in your being. Only this time was different, my mom was still there, yet the same, because cancer has a way of pulling you through the stages of grief just the same. The same bittersweet push and pull I felt with the parents during Student Orientation and then with myself.

The rawness. You are stripped of everything you once knew, and you're only left with what is. Reassessment is only natural.

Who am I? What do I believe? Where do I go from here? This is the third time; shouldn't this be easier by now? Oh, dear God, just take the pain away.

Channeling that pain and power into something more.

Hanging on yet letting go.

*"There is a healing light in this world,
a healing spirit more powerful
than any darkness we may encounter."*

– Mother Teresa

chapter ten

FINDING THE LIGHT

"Is it me?" I questioned, wondering if I was inherently unemployable. "There has to be more than this in life. I'm comfortable. I'm grateful to have a good job, decent benefits, and I'm good at what I do. I've checked off all the boxes. I should be *happy*, so why am I not?"

It was true. I was comfortable, complacent even. But definitely not happy. It was October 2014, a little over a year after mom's hospitalization. She had just completed her year of chemo and thankfully was officially in remission. However, with her tumor, they know it will grow back; it's just a matter of when. Things were pretty much back to "normal" with my parents; dad finishing harvest and my mom settling into the holiday routine. Matt's family was still in Indiana and to be honest, I can't remember the last time I talked to him on the phone. Normal to the degree that life went back to pre-diagnosis, but post-accident. The middle ground of surviving, not thriving.

I had been in my "dream job" at the university for two years now, yet something was missing. I tried my hand at a side hustle of a multi-level marketing (MLM) business to fulfill that pull for something more, yet it didn't align. My boys were growing by the day and I was in an endless cycle of a 5:30 a.m. workout, daycare drop-off, work at an energy-draining job, pick up boys, make supper, bedtime routine, and start my second job at 8:30

p.m. Cycle, rinse, repeat. There was no joy and I certainly wasn't present. I was constantly living for the next big thing and not truly witnessing the blessings that were in front of me.

"You deserve to be happy," Renée answered on the other end of the phone.

Moments passed as I checked and rechecked the list of gratefulness in my head and yet it wasn't adding up. "I can't just sit and let life pass me by," I continued. "I don't know what it is, but the thought of staying where I am makes me sick. There has to be more to life."

Thoughts of continuing on in higher education felt misaligned and so melancholy. I had searched for other jobs in the area, but none of those felt right, either. *Why is this so hard?* I thought. *Surely I'm not the only one who wants more to life than this.* The urge to watch my boys grow and creating my own life on my terms resonated so much more, yet I had no idea how to do that. I witnessed others growing through their MLM and finding financial peace, but I knew I wanted and needed more than that. Something was bubbling inside.

"Kathryn, it's perfectly okay to outgrow an organization and to go after what you want. The real question is, what do you want?"

Whoa. What a loaded question, I thought. *Nobody has asked me that before.* Deep down I felt a shift. It had been mounting for some time and I kept pushing it back down, not wanting to admit it. After a moment of silence, I genuinely shared my heart albeit barely above a whisper, "I want to tell my story."

I could hear her smile on the other end of the phone. Sensing her excitement, she said, "I've been waiting a long time to hear that. Alright kid, let's tell your story."

Renée was such a prominent role model in my life personally and professionally; and has been since my accident. She was the second mom who stood at arms' length to watch me grow from afar, just to swoop in when I needed her the most. She was right there after Nathan, Mark, and even dropped everything to hold my hand after my mom's impending diagnosis along with treading the uneasy waters of motherhood. Renée also was the one who helped me navigate the professional world, as she inspired me to go back to college and every job offer I received, I passed it by her first. I looked up to her on every account.

"How?" I asked, unsure of who or how I would share my story or find a job that would let me do so. At the ripe age of 29, I still wasn't sure what I wanted to be when I grew up. I just knew there had to be more than surviving.

"How about this, come to my Speaker Summit," replied Renée. "It's for my team of speakers, but I want you there."

"What? No, I can't," I said, taken aback knowing how much I would be putting her out. *I'm just looking for guidance, not a hand out*, I thought. "We really can't afford it. We're barely making ends meet right now, there's no way I can drop this on Aaron."

"No, it's on me," she replied confidently. "It's my Summit, I make the rules and I want you there. I am awarding you a scholarship to attend, because I believe in you. If you can swing the hotel, everything else will be taken care of."

A huge sense of relief washed over me and I found myself silently crying with gratitude. "Are you sure?" I asked in between sobs.

"You want to tell your story?" asked Renée. "Then this is how we start. You'll learn from the best."

I hung up the phone and let the tears fall. Emotions ranging from excitement to being petrified to nervousness back to gratitude and everything in between. My thoughts followed suit. *I'm going to be a speaker! Oh my god, I don't know how to speak. What will everyone think? I won't know anyone there. Will they know I was gifted this beautiful opportunity? How will they know? I'm a natural in front of a classroom and I've been on stage in front of plenty of audiences, how hard can it be? Fuck, what if I suck? What if I'm one of those speakers that goes into high school lyceums that everyone hates? What if I waste Renée's time and money? But what if I don't?*

Oh my God, I'm going to be a speaker!

• • •

Overcome with a mix of excitement, extreme shyness, and a bit of nausea, I walked into the room for the Speaker Summit Meet & Greet. The three-hour drive there, I prayed and gave myself a pep talk of how I was supposed to be here. Everything was leading up to that moment.

The Summit was held at a quaint lodge in the heart of lakes country in Minnesota. It was a three-day retreat for seasoned and new speakers learning the art of the business side of speaking. Renée had brought her team with leaders in marketing, social media, business plans, along with photography and videography. The weekend was packed with in-depth sessions and I was coming in with a feeling of inadequateness, yet open to the experience. I didn't know what to expect, but I knew this was a gift of a lifetime, so I was going all in whatever the stakes were.

I soaked in everything about the room and the women as I looked around. We sat in a semi-circle and I found it intriguing at the mix of ages and backgrounds that I saw. These friendly faces, these smiles...this isn't so bad, I thought, trying to calm my nerves. Fifteen women came from all over the Midwest to attend and learn from Renée, an internationally renowned humorous speaker. They were leaders in healthcare, agriculture, spiritual practices, mental health, and all had an inspirational message to share for female audiences.

I leaned in, taking advantage of learning about these women and their backstories. I appreciated their vulnerability and ease when it came to sharing, something I desperately wanted to have. I read their body language and had keen perception as to who knew each other and who was a newbie just like me.

As we went around introducing ourselves, I found myself getting more and more brave about what I was going to say. I had been practicing it my pep talk as I was driving to the Summit. I loved hearing from the other participants and found more connections that we had in common versus not. When it got to my turn, I bravely jumped in for the first time. *Don't forget to breathe*, I thought to myself.

"Hey ya'll, I'm Kathryn. I'm not a speaker, yet, but I think I'm going to be. I guess I'm here to learn from all of you and to really dig in and see where I belong in the speaking world," I said, taking a deep breath before going all in. "See, I was in a tragic car accident at the age of 15, lost my brother in another car accident at the age of 19, and last year my mom was diagnosed with a brain tumor. I have a story to tell, so I guess I'm here to learn how to share it."

I exhaled and looked around the room. Even opening myself up just that little crack let my true self shine through, albeit dimly. It was the first time that I had acknowledged my hurtful past to anyone not in my immediate circle, let alone a group of strangers. Just from that tiny snippet, I felt the support and smiles from across the room. I couldn't hold it together any longer. I broke open and the tears fell. A sweet release where, for the first time, felt others hold space for me; something I wholeheartedly welcomed.

"Oh my gosh, I'm so sorry! I don't know why my face is leaking!" I joked, wiping the tears away to get off any trace of vulnerability. *Get your shit together, Kathryn*, I critically thought to myself. *If you act like the blubbering mess of the group, everyone will think you are.*

"No, don't be sorry," Renée said. "It's okay to let them fall.

It's time to open up and share. You're safe here." I looked around to the others who all smiled in agreement. One gal even reached over to squeeze my hand and offer a wink in solidarity. The light that was reflected back to me from the other women in the room reassured me that I was safe, and this was the first step in finding my way. Finally.

As the night went on, some of us stayed back and took our conversations to the bar where we cracked open a bit more. Stories of loss, cancer, divorce, miracles, and babies all crossed the table between four of us. There was a sense of connection and divine synchronicity at how our lives paralleled each other for being complete strangers. We all had the same story, just in different words. I found it very cathartic and vulnerable to openly admit, me too! Something I had been searching for far too long.

I walked back up to my room later looking forward to a full night's sleep without interruption, smiling at how life-changing the weekend was going to be. I crawled into my bed and took out my journal. My gratitude list overflowed as my pen hit the paper.

First on the list: *That I survived. That I'm here to tell my story.*

• • •

"How are you doing?" Renée asked me during a scheduled break during our second session the next day. "You've been quiet."

"Overwhelmed," I confessed. "But so good! I'm taking it all in. And I'm quiet because I don't know what questions to ask at this point." *That's partly true,* I thought. *I am so scared to disappoint you and I don't feel worthy of being here that I am sinking back into my chair hoping to disappear.*

"You're glad you're here though?" she asked, reassuringly. "It's a good group of women, isn't it?

"Absolutely, I'm 100% glad I'm here," I replied, trying to be enthusiastic. "It just feels right." More thoughts of guilt and unworthiness started creeping into my head, but I pushed them down with the rest of my emotions and pushed forward. I found my seat again and was reflecting on the day so far. I was intentional in getting outside of my comfort zone and converse with everybody in the room. Not one for surface or casual conversation, I loved digging in deep and hearing their stories and reflections of their experiences. It was a great mix of ages, backgrounds, professions, and speaking experience. I was soaking it all in when I felt someone walk up behind me. Looking behind my shoulder, I saw Joy's kind eyes and gentle smile.

Joy was a healer and worked with multiple energy modalities with her clients. She previously worked at the same university as I did and even worked with a close friend and coworker of mine, but we did not know each other before meeting this weekend. I had heard a lot about her, but I was so scared to meet her because of her abilities. *She can read you like a book without you ever saying a word*, Grace told me about Joy. *She is amazingly powerful, so one needs to be ready to work with her.* That thrilled and frightened me.

Even in just the first few sessions of the group that morning, I had witnessed Joy sharing some intuitive insight with others in the room and was amazed at how spot on she was for their journey. Her presence was magnetic, and I was strangely drawn to her. It scared me, yet I was so intrigued. Joy was also one of the four who stayed late last night and heard the details of my story. With her questions, it was like she opened the spigot and instead, I turned into a well.

"I wanted to share something with you," she gently said, holding a cocktail napkin in her hand. Somewhat knowing where she was going, I took a deep breath, giddy and breathless that it was my turn to receive some wisdom of my new journey, my new path. Joy looked me straight in the eyes. "I want you to know that your brother has been here the entire time, watching over you right here," she said as she waved her hand over my right shoulder.

Wait, what? Taken aback, I did not expect this type of wisdom. I mean, I had always felt a connection to Mark and knew he was always present, but I was not prepared to have someone confirm that. Plus, everyone else who had received guidance from Joy was more business related... not receiving messages from the dead.

"He is quite the character," she continued, not registering that I was not putting all the dots together yet. "Full of expressions and side remarks. She then laughed and said, "And he swears a lot."

Oh my God. Oh my God. Oh my god. My wide eyes held back the tears. I was so overcome with emotion yet felt so at peace.

"For fuck's sake, of course he's here," I laughed, confirming Mark's presence. "And you're absolutely right, that's exactly the way Mark is. Full of piss and vinegar."

Joy laughed and exclaimed, "He couldn't help himself! He was getting so worked up over you... I had a hard time concentrating because it was almost comedic to watch!" She mimicked what actions he was doing. "These are the four things he kept repeating about you," she continued, looking down to her note on the napkin and then handing it to me.

1. *Spitfire*
2. *Has so much more to say than she realizes*
3. *Heart based*
4. *So much bigger than her stature*

As Joy went on to explain the comments in more detail, but I was awestruck at the accuracy and detail of what she was saying. "Right now you're acting so meek and mild, but you're usually a spitfire; that you can hold your own and this isn't you... you're shrinking back," she relayed. "He kept pacing back and forth saying that you have so much to say, and yet you have kept quiet this whole time. Not just here, but in life."

My entire life, I thought. I agreed whole-heartedly and confirmed what Joy was relaying from Mark.

She continued, "He says you need to speak from the heart, that everything you have been wanting to say, you just need to say it and people will listen."

No more holding back, Kathryn.

"Lastly, he kept referring to how much bigger you are than you appear. Not your stature or physical sense, but in the sense of your presence. Does that resonate?"

I could just hear him calling me Chubbs, my nickname he used when referring to how big I was as his "little" sister.

"Yes, oh my God, yes," I exclaimed, my mind spinning. *What does this even mean? Why here? Why now?* "I can't even think straight right now, but holy shit…that resonates completely!" Deep down I always knew Mark and I had an unbreakable bond, even if we were in different dimensions. I had felt his presence known, and the more I dug into my spirituality and personal development, I saw his nods from heaven via feathers, songs, and dreams. But to have heard words from his mouth? I was awestruck.

I was pulled out of my trance as Renée breezed back up to the front to jump back into the next session and Joy took her place back across the room. I tried to concentrate on the next session, but rather I found myself sneaking looks at Joy trying to see if she was connecting with Mark over my shoulder again. In a short five-minute break, my whole world was rocked. That small confirmation of Mark's presence planted a seed of healing I didn't know I needed.

• • •

Throughout the weekend, I found myself pulled towards Joy, drawn into anything she said; hanging on every word. Synchronicities revealed themselves, guiding us together in focus groups, sitting next to each other at supper, and even providing feedback on the last day for our keynotes. But it wasn't until the Summit was over that Joy asked for me to accompany her back to her room as she had something for me. When we walked into her room, I was overcome with a deep sense of gratitude for this weekend. I still had no idea what it all meant, however the weekend confirmed I was exactly right where I needed to be.

"I want you to read this," she said as she handed me a book. "It's a quick read, but I think you will find that the lessons will resonate on a whole different level for you."

"Like how?" I questioned, curious as to what she meant by a different level.

"It's about communicating with the Divine. How God works in mysterious ways and how we can raise our vibrations and connect with our guides, angels, and our higher self," she explained. "I know you're ready to learn more. I can feel it."

"Yes, absolutely," I responded, knowing that I had turned the corner of my faith and spirituality. This whole weekend had opened me wider than I had ever experienced before, personally and professionally. The spark had been lit.

"I want you to know that I can see great things in your future," Joy continued. "Wherever you go, please know that you are protected and being guided every step of the way...even when it doesn't feel like it."

Tears were welling in my eyes as I let her words soak in.

"Thank you," I said. "That means a lot to me. I can feel it, too. I just wish I knew where I was going." So much doubt plagued my every step, wanting it to be perfect. This one was no exception. I wanted to be a speaker and yet, still had so much work to do before getting there.

"Trust the journey. This is just the beginning," Joy continued, referring to honoring my past and using it to ignite my future. "If you'd like, I would be honored to work with you and assist in your healing. When you're ready, that is."

"I would like that very much," I responded, feeling a sense of relief knowing I was on the right path. "I feel like I'm on the cusp of something big, yet it scares me. I'm not sure that I'm quite there yet." Joy just smiled, not saying a word but I could feel her energy gave me the confirmation I needed. "I am so thankful for your friendship and healing presence this weekend," I said. "I need some time, but once I'm ready, you'll be the first call."

I believed in her gifts yet was scared of them. I knew she could see more than she was letting on and I wasn't sure I was ready to dive in deep yet. This weekend cracked me open far more than I ever anticipated, and I wasn't ready to use a pry bar and dig in further.

"Whenever you are ready, I will be here for you," Joy said, then gazed past my shoulder again and smiled. "And Mark says *it's about fucking time*."

• • •

After the Summit ended, I drove away from the resort and all that transpired in the three days away, overcome with emotion. I felt pride for following my heart, happiness in hearing from Mark, excitement for a future in speaking, anxiousness to return home to real life with the boys, and an overwhelming sadness at how long it has been since I closed off part of my heart.

Tears streamed down my face for the 15-mile drive on the lone, two-lane highway that rolled across the prairie until I hit the major highway. Thankfully, I didn't pass more than three vehicles the entire way, as it took all of me to keep my eyes open and on the road. I struggled to find enough tissues between wiping my eyes and catching my runny nose. I thought I had finally found composure when the next song from my iPhone streamed through the radio.

As soon as the piano and guitar strummed the first notes flooded into my ears a wave of emotion crashed over me so hard that I pulled over to the side of the road. By the time the lyrics came on I was parked and sobbing to *Freebird* by Lynard Skynard in the middle of nowhere in central Minnesota.

"Mark" I sighed. "I feel you, I know you're here." I continued to ride out that wave and soon I managed to smile, even laugh, through my tears. Mark always managed to show up right when I needed him to. I sat in wonder of what this all meant. Grateful. Blessed. Brokenly beautiful to have lived this hard life. Knowing full well that God intended to use me for great things.

The next day after coming home from the Summit, I grabbed my coffee and walked right into my coworker Grace's office.

● ● ●

She looked up from her computer and greeted me. "Hey babe! How was it?"

With big eyes, I gushed, "I met her. Joy, I met her! Oh my God, and she saw Mark!" I threw the cocktail napkin with her note written on it onto Grace's desk. "Look! This is what he said!" Still in disbelief, I could hardly contain my excitement and shock at what all transpired over the weekend.

Grace's soft and reassuring smile made me ease into my chair. "Pretty incredible, right? She definitely has a gift. How does this make you feel? Wait, tell me about the entire thing... start from the beginning and do not leave a single detail out."

I proceeded to describe in detail the entire weekend. My nerves, my reservations, my ah-ha moments, and my new-found confidence in being onto something bigger than myself with speaking. "This is the start of *something*," I said. "I can feel it. I have something to say... I just need to find that voice and share it."

After I got done, Grace leaned back. "Wow, that's incredible!" said Grace, with a sense of wonder. "Can you imagine? You know there's more to life than these four walls. You are going to go places, you know that? I can feel it."

"I want to work with Joy, but I'm scared. Were you scared?" I asked. "Like, I've never been to therapy."

"Wait, what?" Grace said, astonished. "Haven't you talked to anyone about everything that you've gone through?"

A bit taken aback, I sheepishly, "No. I guess I talked to a grief counselor once after Mark died, but she was a client of mine when I did hair and she worked at a funeral home in town with families during the burial process. But no, nothing other than that."

Grace leaned in more and out of genuine concern, asked, "How did you deal with the physical and emotional grief of your accident? And then to lose your brother so close afterward, that must have brought up something in you, no? You didn't talk to anyone?"

Embarrassed at this point, I looked down and stammered over my words. "I guess I talked to Aaron. And I journaled. I channeled my grief and instead of dwelling on the pain, I turned it into something I was thankful for each day." I looked up at Grace and shrugged. "I guess I was too mad at Nathan that I shut

161

that door and never bothered to open it up again. And then when Mark died, I wasn't mad at him, so I grieved differently. I used his death as the vehicle to get me here, today."

"I'm just amazed that your mom didn't drag your ass into a therapist's office! Hell, I brought my girls in after their father was diagnosed as terminal. I didn't know how to answer questions and our therapist was a lifesaver; not only for them but for me."

"Well, fifteen years ago, it's not like therapy was a high priority in small town living. I don't think I even knew what a therapist or counseling even was," I said. "It's not like today where it's a part of overall wellness. They fixed my broken back, it was up to me to fix my broken heart."

"True," responded Grace, thinking carefully of her next words. "Working with Joy will be intense, but in a total loving and healing way. If you think you're ready, I say go for it."

"I don't know if I'm ready," I confessed, after a moment. "But I think it's something that I need. If not to help me share that part of my life, at least for me to process it and be able to talk about it."

"Absolutely," confirmed Grace, startled by her phone ringing for her first appointment of the day. "Now back to real life," she smiled with a wink. "But I'm proud of you! This is going to be big for you."

● ● ●

Joy's office was very zen-like, with a calm color palette and incense and oils burning. It was six weeks after the speaker summit and it was our first appointment together. As she escorted me into her therapy room, I was greeted by a comfy rocker with ottoman and the softest green blanket I had ever touched. It felt like butter and I immediately relaxed into the plush cushions of the chair.

"We are going to get started by getting some background and details of your life," Joy said as she got herself situated in the chair across from me, covering herself with the same kind of blanket, only purple. "Start from the beginning and work your way up to today."

"Well, I grew up on a hog farm outside of Beltrami," I started. "I have two older brothers..." and described myself on autopilot, the way I described myself to acquaintances: skimming over the hard parts and focusing in on the easy parts. Instead of halting the conversation about my accident, which was typical to hear some condolences, instead we paused and discussed my mom's diagnosis and my beliefs of Mark's presence in her recovery.

Thinking we were going forward and work on what was weighing on me, Joy knocked me back a few notches when she said, "Tell me about Nathan."

Caught off guard, I thought carefully before speaking, knowing she saw more than she let on. "I loved him with every fiber of my being," I said with tears in my eyes, seeing his wide smile and bright blue eyes flash in my head. I shook that image loose and sighed, "But he didn't love me the same way. I know a lot of my worthiness issues stem from him."

"What makes you say that?" Joy questioned further.

"Well, he cheated on me. With someone in our class who was a nobody," I blurted out, not mincing words. "He put me on a pedestal and worshipped the ground I walked on, just to fuck me over with her." I couldn't even say her name. The rage boiled inside of me and I could feel the thick, hot tears ready to fall. "I have come to realize that if I wasn't good enough for him and he supposedly loved me, how would I be good enough for anyone?"

Joy sat silently, taking notes and not giving any inclination of her thoughts. She put her notes down and looked me deeply in the eyes. "Do you think that you've fully loved since Nathan?"

"I think so?" questioning now my entire relationship with Aaron. "I mean, I love Aaron. He's my rock, I can't imagine doing life without him."

"Of course you love Aaron," Joy affirmed gently. "But do you feel as if you've loved him the same as you did with Nathan? Without abandon?"

I had to pause for a few moments truly thinking. "I think we have a different kind of love," I confessed. "There is a level of trust and undeniable presence between us that is unshakeable. Not like Nathan where we were always so rocky. Aaron is the strong, steady force that I need in my life. He is my anchor."

"That's amazing that you have that in your life. It sounds like Aaron is good for you," said Joy. "Besides Aaron, do you let others in?"

"Nope," I said matter-of-factly. "Not at all. I bet there are five people in my inner circle that know about my past. I don't talk about it."

"You put a wall around your heart to protect it," Joy said. "The tricky thing about walls is that they don't just keep people out, they also keep people in. Think of Aaron. If you have a wall around your heart, are you giving all of yourself to him?"

My eyes widened with the realization of what I had done for the past fifteen years. I had limited my heart and love to Aaron without knowing it. The wall that I created to protect me also was breaking me.

"How do I stop?" I asked, wanting to hammer down the wall immediately for Aaron's sake.

"You decide to tear down the wall, brick by brick," Joy replied. That comment hit me to the core. The thought of being open and vulnerable terrified me, yet a part of me longed for that liberation.

"While we've been talking, I called out to Nathan to see if he would make his presence known," she started. "But Mark came through loud and clear, instead. It seems as if he won't let Nathan through."

I chuckled with the tears in my eyes, half rolling them in disbelief. "Of course Mark won't let him through," I said. "Knock it off, Mark."

"Mark wants to know if you're sure?" Joy asked. "He's blocking Nathan coming through unless you're sure. Apparently he's been doing this the entire time."

"I'm sure," I confirmed, holding my breath. I knew I needed this more than Mark's protection. I intently watched Joy as she used her gifts to channel Nathan. I watched for a confirmation, but I didn't need to, I felt the shift instead. I could feel his presence, as it was totally different than Mark's. A duality of spirits, as Mark's presence did not leave the room; as if his big brother duties were still intact.

"Nathan, he had soulful eyes, didn't he?" Joy asked. "And almost a playful presence about him? Not playful like Mark, but youthful, almost? A very handsome face. Very handsome." Smiling, I confirmed it was, indeed, him. I knew it the moment I felt the shift in the room. Nathan still had that magnetic pull about him. "Mark said he's not going anywhere," Joy chuckled. "It's almost as if he's standing in the corner with his arms crossed." Not sure where she was headed, I kept my eyes fixated on Joy.

Logically I couldn't explain it, but I could feel the different energies in the room. My mind and soul somewhat at odds trying to understand everything that was unfolding. I felt cautious to trust in what was happening but compelled to open more to the mystery.

"Nathan wants you to know that he never meant to hurt you," Joy started. "That although you were connected on a soul level, he was still human and still made mistakes. She was a mistake.

You, however, were his muse, and yes, he kept you on a pedestal. You are still there, actually." I stayed quiet, still fixated on Joy. She was quiet as she received messages and tried to compute them. "Mark is quite the protector. He is asking Nathan that if he really loved you, he wouldn't have hurt you this much for this long."

I was trying to picture two spirits yelling at each other, envisioning both Mark and Nathan in their human forms, only angelic-like. I found myself audibly laughing through the tears.

"Nathan confirms that he never meant to hurt your heart like this, but he kept true on his promise to not have anything hurt you," Joy continued. Interjecting her own perception, Joy smiled and said, "It sounds like you have two very protective guardian angels. Nathan is saying that you need to forgive yourself; that you've been holding onto this for far too long. He takes responsibility for himself and asks that you not only forgive him, but even more so, forgive yourself. None of this was your fault."

Upon hearing those words, I closed my eyes and the hot tears fall silently down my face. Releasing all of that anger, all of that hurt in one instant. Forgiveness. I felt the weight from fifteen years of carrying that hurt lift off my chest; as if I could take a deep breath for the first time in those fifteen years.

"Yes, I know this," I said, feeling the weight dissipate and letting the light back in.

"You have carried this for far too long," Joy reiterated. "You are whole. You are worthy. You are so extremely blessed! It's time to sit in that light and just be."

Just be. Her words pierced my soul, slicing into the depths that I hadn't felt in years. I felt the shift; the quantum shift that my life from that moment on would be forever changed for the better. In that moment, I committed to heal the soul fracture that I had been ignoring for past 15 years and choosing to use my soul lessons to help heal others. This crucial groundwork that I created with Joy was the catalyst in a long journey of restoring my soul and releasing what no longer served me. In just a few sessions that we had together, it confirmed something that I had known the whole time: I was made for more.

• • •

In the two additional sessions that I had with Joy, I fell head over heels with the idea of healing modalities through Angels and the spirit world; communicating with God through His lightworkers. Our sessions brought forth clarity and unexpected revelations in my everyday, ordinary life. Hints and messages from Heaven everywhere I looked, and even when I least expected it.

It was an ordinary Saturday where the boys and I just got home from coffee with my mom and I was getting lunch ready. As any parent, I was good at working at a level of constant commotion to the point where it feels lonely or quiet in an empty house or car. The noise level was always at a constant Level 7 all the time.

As the boys were down the hall washing up and chatting away, I was busy doing my own thing. Out of nowhere I am taken aback as I overhear James down the hall saying a word that stopped me in my tracks.

"What did you say?" I asked, holding my breath.

He stopped and looked at me straight in the eyes and confidently replied, "Gorgeous!"

It was the first time I had heard that word from a boy in 15 years.

"Where did you hear that?" I asked, trying to figure out why or how he was throwing out random adjectives for a 3-year-old to know.

"Gor-jusssss," he replied with a smile, emphasizing the grand scale of the word.

"Buddy, did you learn that at school?" I asked more pointedly.

"Nope," he said, walking to the counter where his lunch sat ready to eat.

Following his lead, I asked, "Did you hear that on TV?"

"Nope," he replied nonchalantly, not picking up my heightened anticipation for what I already knew.

"Then where did you learn that word?"

"I dreamed it," he said, taking a bite of his chicken nugget.

"Tell me more about your dream," I inquired more, trying not to press too hard. James could always tell when being pressed for information and would shut down easily, even at the age of three.

"I dunno," he said. "There was a boy and an owl, and they talked to me and they kept saying that. Gor-juss." He smiled so sweetly at me, not realizing how I was choking back tears.

"Neat! Wow, do you remember what the boy looked like? Or what else he or the owl said?" I knew I was pressing my luck at the memory of a 3-year-old, but I was willing to take the chance.

"No, not really. He had dark hair like daddy, but he was not daddy. They knew you, though."

A sense of familiarity and wonder washed over me. I smiled and told James, "That sounds nice. I bet I knew them, too." There was no way to explain to a 3-year-old that Nathan came to him in a dream, shortly after I opened up that part of my life again. To hear that word, even from my own baby, gave me a hug from the other side.

chapter eleven

....

CHANGING SEASONS

M y therapy and healing started with Joy, but certainly did not end there. I dove into as much personal development as I could get my hands on, along with harnessing my own intuition. I dove into the thoughts and inspirations of my favorite authors, became enlightened by new ideas and new influencers. I didn't shed an old way of thinking, rather, I expanded my thoughts into bigger beliefs and harnessed a truth that resonated on a soul level. Books, podcasts, online summits, along with investing in courses, workshops, and coaches broadened my horizons versus the traditional landscape that I became much too familiar with.

I had always felt connected to God, but my faith and intuition grew exponentially more once I fully immersed myself into it. Not one to shy away from paving my own way, I opened myself up to new opportunities and went after them. Not feeling supported in my typical 9-5 job, I knew there was more to learn and be.

Fortunately, I had a dear friend who was on the same journey as me. Grace's life and my life were parallel on a number of factors; growing up as farm kids in rural Minnesota, losing a loved one too early in life, and left with a shattered heart and learning how to piece it back together. She was actually the one who opened my eyes wider to spirituality than what the Catholic Church ever did yet demonstrated how they can live synonymously. A perfect blend of tradition and New Age consciousness.

I walked into Grace's office one day and placed two books I had borrowed on her cabinet. I sat down, across from her as she leaned back in her chair. Behind her was mixed artwork between her three daughters and her favorite artist. A strong blended message of courage, living your best life, and embracing your wings to fly. Grace's corner office was located two down from mine, yet I felt like I was in her office more than my own contemplating the meaning of life in between assisting students. How to live, be, and give more.

"You look different today," Grace said. "Your energy is different, which makes you look different."

"Do I look like a new person?" I joked, making a grand gesture around my face.

"No, but something is different," she said. "What did you think?" referencing to the books I just brought back.

"Deep. Intense. But I liked it...a lot," I responded. "Some of it I knew, I think. It resonated more deeply than learning something new. Does that make sense?"

"Absolutely," she affirmed. "You're remembering. You knew it all before, it's just coming back now."

"Right. I like that," I said, thinking out loud. "Speaking of which, I had an intense dream last night. I think it had to do with therapy wrapping up."

"Tell me more," Grace said, genuinely interested. She always had a way of never making me feel crazy when digging in deeper to decipher seemingly inoculate messages.

"Well, you know I had my last session with Joy and I cried the whole way home. Like, literally sobbed," I confessed. "I shouldn't have been driving. It was intense all that I released."

"It was years of emotion that came out," Grace expressed as she swept her short golden blonde hair out of her eye. She then smiled and said, "Finally forgiving years' worth of anger has a way of doing that. I would only expect it to be intense."

"True," I said. "I woke up feeling lighter than I have in years. Actually, I don't remember not ever carrying that weight around with me." I motioned a lifting off my chest, like I could fully breathe again. I was unaware at how much extra weight the baggage from my accident had accumulated; ultimately weighing down on my spirit and my soul.

It was finally forgiving myself, I thought. Forgiving myself finally set me free.

"But my dream," I pressed on. "You know I don't dream very often...like at all. But last night, it was crystal clear. I was in Beltrami and the wind picked up. I looked at the clouds and knew a storm was coming. But instead of going inside, I grabbed the boys and suddenly we were in our backyard here in town and went out to the dike facing to the West. We were on top of the hill where we could see for miles and miles, and that's when I saw them."

Grace was on the edge of her seat, leaning forward on her desk staring straight at me.

"Four tornadoes," I continued. "Like on the *Wizard of Oz*. All weaving and wreaking havoc. I saw them blowing up dirt and dust and moving closer. I felt the boys holding onto me as if they were scared, but no one said a word. And then all of a sudden, the tornados switched directions. It's like they finally saw me and decided to back down. I watched them blow off into the distance and I took the boys' hands and we walked home."

"How did you feel in the dream and when you woke?" asked Grace, wide-eyed with energy.

173

"Not scared one bit," I replied. "Peaceful, almost. And like I said, I felt like the world had been lifted once I woke. I released it all."

"Whoa. That's powerful!" Grace exclaimed, leaning back into her chair again after a few moments of processing what I had just said. "Four tornadoes. What does the number four mean?" She started Googling. "The number four represents the four elements: Air, Fire, Water, Earth," Grace started reading from her computer screen. "That makes sense with it being a tornado," she said looking at me from the corner of her eye. Getting back to her research she read, "And with the energies of the *Archangels!* Yes! You are so protected!"

She continued paraphrasing what she found, "Angel Number 4 indicates your angels are around you and to call upon them when you need help... trust that you have the skills, talents, and abilities to overcome obstacles to achieve highest aspirations... and the Universe works in your favor to establish solid foundations and advance you along your path!"

"Kathryn! Do you know what this means?" exclaimed a wide-eyed Grace.

"I think so?" I sheepishly answered, not knowing where she'd take it.

"Well, what caused the big release that you had yesterday?"

"I forgave myself," I answered, holding back a few tears.

"Your tornadoes signified all the dirt and debris you've been carrying around in your heart has been blown out by forgiving yourself. The four tornadoes signified change and chaos and stress and holding onto past hurt. They collided and moved, but they shifted away from you. Forgiving yourself changed all that."

"I know, right?" I responded, sitting back in disbelief. "That's totally what it is!"

"That's why you look different!" Grace said as she clapped her hands with fervor. "I knew it!"

"I guess so," I laughed at her big ah-ha. "Maybe by the time I'm done with this soul lesson from my accident, I'll totally be a different person."

"Most people are," she smiled, pressing further. "The real question is, what are you going to do with it?"

"I don't know?" I questioned out loud. "It needs to percolate a bit more. It will present itself when the time is right, I suppose."

"It will," she confirmed. "And you'll know exactly what to do next."

• • •

I looked around for my mom as the boys and I walked into the crowded coffee shop. There she sat, patiently waiting in a large booth by herself, which made her look so petite and fragile. It was April 2015 and I was coming off a hard morning getting both boys out the door. Naturally, we were late, as James lost a shoe and Drew refused to go potty before we had to leave. For priding myself on punctuality, these boys notched my Type A personality down to a B-minus. Learning how to roll on their terms versus my own had been a hard power struggle.

My mom's eyes lit up as she smiled when she saw the boys and they excitedly ran to her for a hug. Saturday mornings were synonymous for coffee dates and grandmas as growing up, as I did the same thing at the Beltrami Mall Café with my grandma. I always looked forward to having a reprieve on Saturday mornings after a long week of balancing work and boys.

"Grandma!" Drew exclaimed as he weaved around people's legs to get to her faster.

"Hey there, Drewbear!" my mom answered, wrapping him up in a big hug. James was up next, followed by me.

"Hey, Babe!" my mom said.

"Late, as usual," I replied, harboring some resentment at how I couldn't get it together. My mind wandered back to the missing shoe and the escapade of finding it. It was found under the couch, naturally.

"Oh, don't even worry," she smiled, motioning up to the counter. "Let's have coffee." We settled back into our booth, the boys taking turns to tell Grandma about daycare and preschool shenanigans from the week. I felt relieved to keep the focus off of me, as I was contemplating how to break the news to my mom. The past two times this didn't go over well, but I knew I couldn't keep it a secret much longer.

I was pregnant.

Soon the boys got bored of talking and found Chutes and Ladders to occupy the time, which in reality it meant fighting over who goes first and how to play. At ages 3 and 4, attention spans and tempers were short. *This is it*, I thought. I opened my mouth to start talking when my mom beat me to it.

"Well, I had my scan on Thursday," my mom started.

"Yep," I said, not thinking much of it. Her scans were a routine procedure for her brain tumor study, conducted through the cancer center. Every three months she goes in for an hour-long MRI, followed by a cognitive test and blood work. She then meets with the oncologist and social worker to discuss any changes or elements from the baseline conducted after her craniotomy.

"They found a growth," she said matter-of-factly, her manicured hands wrapped around her coffee mug.

I slowly swallowed and looked up from the boys playing into my mom's eyes, which were brimmed with tears. "What?" I asked numbly, unsure of how to process.

"It's a spot about the size of the tip of my pinky," she explained, hands still held tightly around the mug, as if she didn't know what else to do with them.

"What does this mean?" I asked. *No. Not again. There's nothing left for treatment*, I thought. *I can't do this again.*

"No treatment right now," she said, trying to reassure my unspoken thoughts. "We're just going to watch it. It's too small for radiation even if I could get it." She had the highest dose of radiation initially after her diagnosis, so she was told that if the tumor ever came back, chemo would be the only viable option for treatment. "We'll just wait and see."

"Oh," I said, still numb. I looked down at my two babies sitting in the booth next to her, holding back tears, barely being able to breathe. *It's not supposed to be like this. We've already done this once*, I thought. *Not again.*

"My doctor gave me a prescription of 'go out and live'," she kept going. "So that's what I'm going to do. I can't sit and wallow. I wanted to see you and my boys, so here I am." She smiled and squeezed James sitting next to her. *Oh my God, the irony of all this. This whole picture. She looks fine, she acts fine, and yet it's not. It's crumbling again*, I thought.

Not one to hang onto a hard subject, she switched gears and asked, "Are you going anywhere after this?"

"No, I think I'm just going to head home," I replied. *Where else would I go after an announcement like this?* Thoughts and emotions were still swirling throughout my body. *How does one just continue to go on like nothing has happened? That nothing has changed?*

"Okay," she said as the boys were getting more and more restless. An hour was a long time for little boys to sit still in a booth, and today they were extra rambunctious. A sure sign that they picked up on the tension and uneasy energy that just transpired.

"Thanks for having coffee with me, boys!" my mom said as she got high fives from the boys. "I'll see you next week?"

"Okay!" they both chirped back, unaffected by my mom's news. They didn't remember her being sick. They hardly remembered visiting her in the hospital or her with short or no hair. Thankfully, they never witnessed the fog or sickness that followed her chemo treatment. Even if she wasn't feeling well, she always put on a good show for the short time we visited. As we said our goodbyes and piled back into the car, I watched as my mom drove away. That's when I lost it.

Slumped over the steering wheel, I sobbed in the front seat. A visceral reaction to the news that I just encountered, a wave of anger and betrayal by God washed over me. My tears mixed with uncontrollable shaking and almost a PTSD reaction of hitting rock bottom again. Only this time, I had extra hormones contributing to my uncontainable drowning of tears.

Not again, I thought. *I can't do this again. How am I supposed to focus on the life forming within me when my life is deteriorating around me? This is not how this is supposed to go.*

"Mama?" I heard from the backseat. "Can we go home?"

"Yes, baby," I said trying to be strong, albeit unsuccessful. I still have two, well, three babies to take care of. Tears streamed down as I put the car into drive and started out of the parking lot. Oblivious to the outside world, my thoughts consumed me.

I need my mom. I'm pregnant. I can't do this life without her. I just got her back. I can't lose her again. I need her. I turned to begging. *This is my mom, God. You can't take her. Not like this, not after she's been to hell and back.*

Then, a voice of reason came to me. *If you need her, go to her.* Sitting at a stoplight on the route back home, I decided to turn. A few miles away I found myself in front of the drop-in daycare. I dropped the boys off and called my mom.

"Where are you at?" I asked when she answered.

"I just left Macy's and am going out to the garden center," she replied. "Why?"

"I just dropped the boys off at drop-in. I'll meet you there," I said.

"Oh good," she said. "See you there."

I hung up the phone and wiped my eyes, swollen and red. As I pulled into the parking lot, I regained a bit of my composure before walking in to find her in the nursery admiring all the new annuals; presumably planning ahead for her well-manicured flower beds. I stood back and soaked in how unshaken she seemed for having this blow dealt to her just two days prior. She looks so small, I thought. *Small, but fierce.*

Drawing strength from that, I approached her, and she turned and smiled at me. "Changed your mind?" she asked.

"I just needed my mom," I said with a lump in my throat and tears brimming again.

"Good," she squeezed my hand and continued down the row of begonias.

...

The harsh reminder of my mom's tumor regrowth that life is much too precious to keep waiting for tomorrow set some major plans in motion. Instead of living in fear and scarcity mindset, I spread my wings and invested myself in more personal development. I took an online course on how to own your story and became personally invested in my own soul's growth.

It was there, in my darkened living room after the boys' bedtime, as I took notes that I saw myself reflected back in the author's lessons of addictions, feelings of loss, grieving, old stories of self-limiting beliefs, and trauma. Through the journaling prompts and reflections, that's when the lightbulb moment hit.

If I could heal through a reflection of someone else's tragedy and trauma, why couldn't someone heal through my story? I thought. Not only own my story but share it. I knew I wasn't there yet, as my healing was much too fresh, but I knew that one day, that would be me on stage sharing my truth and at the book signings hugging readers who knew it and felt it. *This is where I'm supposed to be*, I thought.

Not one to ever take the simple path, I blazed my own trail to where I wanted to go. No more feeling stuck or stagnant or complacent, I decided to use my wings that I knew were there.

Next came conversations with Renée about an impending part-time job to learn more about the speaking business from the back end. Those simmering conversations gave me life while the university job that I once loved grew more and more toxic. My lifeline and partner in crime Grace had left six months prior and by this time, I became a hermit in my office. *Keep my head low and survive* was my motto, so I didn't have to engage in office or university politics more than I had to.

But one day, as I was recluse to my office, my phone rang with an outside number. Not a stranger to getting calls from online/ distance students, I answered autonomously ready to direct them to our website for resources.

"Is this Kathryn who spoke at the Student Leadership Conference?" a voice at the other end asked.

Taken aback, I leaned in and grabbed my pen. "Yes, this is her," I answered.

"Hello! My name is Marcy Mitchell and my daughter is a student at UND," she continued. "She heard you speak at the Student Leadership Conference and told me all about you!"

"Oh my goodness, yes! I remember her!" I exclaimed. "She is going into Communications, right?" After my presentation, I remembered a cute, young woman coming up and asking for a card. (Of course, I had none on me and wrote down my information in her notebook like the professional I was. Ha!)

"Yes! Oh my gosh, after all of these months, I wasn't sure if you'd remember her," Marcy continued. "Well, she raved about you and the impact you had on the audience, so I had to reach out. I am the Educational Director for Kinderyears Excellence Academy in the Twin Cities and I would like to book you for our professional development day."

My heart started racing and words failed to reach from my brain to my mouth. Awestruck, I said, "Okay!"

"Our professional development day is October 8th, and we have our keynote booked, but would like for you to do two breakout sessions for our staff. They are the managers and lead teachers for all 32 locations of our preschools. Would that date work for you?"

My heart sank. "October 8th?" I confirmed, counting the weeks. Fuck.

"Yes," she replied.

"I would whole-heartedly love to," I answered hesitantly. "I'm checking my calendar and do have the date open, however, I need to let you know that I will be 37 weeks pregnant."

"Oh my! Well by all means, congratulations!" Marcy sincerely said.

"But this is my third, and I have no history of going into labor early," I said eagerly. "I'm willing to take the chance if you are? I will have my husband come with me just in case, and in the event I do have this little guy early, I can guarantee a fantastic replacement."

I heard Marcy laugh on the other end, "I too had three daughters who took their time coming into this world! I have no problem with booking you as long as you're okay with it!"

My heart leapt, and I immediately answered, "Absolutely!"

After the details were ironed out, we hung up and I sat back recounting what just happened. I just booked my first paid speaking event. My soul was soaring, and I couldn't stop smiling. *This is it*, I thought. *I am doing this. Oh my god, I am going to speak professionally!*

Before I picked up my cell to call Aaron and Renée to share the good news, I jumped up from my desk and did a little ditty of a dance to celebrate. As tears of joy streamed down my face I smiled and whispered, *Thank you*, to Mark and my angels who orchestrated it all. It wasn't lost on me how quickly the Universe showed up once I made up my mind to move forward. *It's time*, I thought.

• • •

Balancing life with as a new family of five, two new entrepreneurial ventures, and trying to find myself in the midst of it all hit me light a freight train. It wasn't pretty. Jack was a sweet and happy baby, and from the moment I held him in my arms, I knew he completed our family. Still, I felt the familiar loom of postpartum depression; I witnessed myself sinking in deep.

Aaron had just left his steady income, yet soul- and time-sucking job to venture out on his own six months earlier. I took the risk of quitting my full-time, state benefitted job to working part-time for Renée as her assistant to be home and more present with my boys. Yet, the stress of a new learning curve of being outnumbered by tiny humans, a whole new learning curve of the speaking world, and lack of sleep did a number on me.

I felt like a failure on all accounts. As we moved through the throngs of having a newborn and then three mobile kids, I struggled juggling all of the demands that everyone needed from me. The boys were alive and fed, but I was far from the bright, present mom I had hoped to be. The house and my heart were in a constant state of disarray. I tried to give more of myself individually to all three of my boys, yet it stretched me thin. I thought we could fake it 'til we make it, but I knew we were all sick of faking it when an early morning conversation turned dark on the way to school.

"Look at that gorgeous sunrise," I said brightly one morning, trying to fake enthusiasm to keep the energy light so James and Drew would start the day on a positive note, rather than the sour tone we got out the door on. "Look at all the colors God used. I bet He painted it just for us!" *Reverse psychology always works, right?*

"I don't like it," said a disgruntled James from the backseat.

"What?" I tried turning his attitude around. *Throw me a bone here, kid. I just mustered all of my strength and stamina to strap you into the car after arguing for 25 minutes before we left.*

"I don't like it," James said again. "I wish the sun would never shine."

Oh, my.

"Why not, buddy?" I asked, slightly on edge as to what may follow. *Save this somehow, Kathryn. You're losing him.* "I love how the sun shines. It fills my heart up every morning!"

"Not me," he said. "Nothing fills my heart up."

Uff. I swallowed hard. *This faking it bullshit isn't working anymore; he needs more.*

• • •

"Mister, he needs you," I begged on the phone. Six months had passed from that early morning conversation with James. Aaron was still working over the road, and I was struggling with keeping things afloat at home. "His whole world has been flipped upside down and all he asks for is you."

We had just started James in play therapy to get to the bottom of his increased outbursts at home and now at school. I sobbed over the phone when making that initial appointment, feeling like a failure of a parent that I couldn't help James in the way he required. It wasn't until a month into his appointments that I started to feel like it was the best decision I made; loving him unconditionally to give him the support he needed. Tools to regulate those big emotions and big spirit that filled his little body.

It was that day that we had a breakthrough in James' progress, but it also weighed heavily on me. Many of James' emotional outbursts stemmed from Aaron being gone. Sure, Aaron was more than present emotionally: calls before and after school, FaceTiming to practice spelling words or lines for a program. But James was longing for his dad's physical presence. Hell, we all were.

Yet I couldn't help but wonder if Aaron's physical presence would make such a lasting imprint on James as my dad had on me. James' outbursts and anger paralleled mine at a young age, as I wanted nothing more than to be seen by my dad. Through my own therapy, I uncovered that a lot of my anger stemmed from being emotionally abandoned a young age.

"Kathryn, I'm doing the best I can," Aaron responded, somewhat despondent as he knew how helpless he was thousands of miles away.

"I know you are, Mister," I said. "You're sacrificing so much for us. I just wish there was a way we could make it all work."

Being the very black and white thinker he is, Aaron responded, "Well, we can. If you want me off the road, that means that you have to go back to work, too. There will be more sacrifices to make all of this work. And let's get real; even then, would you be happy?"

I flinched at the thought of going back to work full-time in a corporate job. Finding a daycare, three separate drop-offs and pick-ups, the bewitching hours once we get home while making supper just to crash after bedtime. I loved the flexibility of being an independently contracted writer and speaking at my leisure, so I could be present with my boys. Having complete control over my schedule so it allowed me to volunteer in their classrooms and schedule their appointments with ease, not to mention summers spent outside instead of in daycare.

"No, that wouldn't make me happy," I said quietly. "I just think we need to find a better balance for all of us. Maybe it's bringing the boys to the shop with you on Saturdays? They can play there while you work."

"How well do you work when the boys are right there?" Aaron asked. "It's one thing for a couple of hours when I'm not busy, but I'm usually working on the truck to get it ready for the week. I can't be answering questions or watching them 100% when I need to be focusing on the truck. It's not fair to them or me, Kathryn."

I remained silent.

"Don't you think I'd be home if I had the time to be?" Aaron asked.

"Yes," I said sheepishly, knowing full well it was true. Aaron was an amazing dad, all in when he was home. It was the "when he's home" part that was lacking.

"This is the season that we're in right now," he continued. "We're both new into working for ourselves and having a young family. We are all sacrificing to build the life we know we want."

I knew this deep in my heart, but I found myself stuck on the notion of how life was supposed to look like versus what it truly was. In the past, I had identified myself and thrived on the archetypes I constructed: student, professional, wife, mother, friend. At that moment, I didn't know who I was. I didn't want to be just a mom or just a wife or just a busy career woman.

So, I started looking for another version of myself, one that represented this new phase in my life. Surprisingly, I found it on the yoga mat of all places. I took a step back from developing myself through courses and coaches and decided to give myself some grace and take it one day at a time. In all the areas of my life that I needed to give up control, it was in asking for help. I convinced Aaron that with the little money we had leftover each month to hire a nanny as my reprieve, even if it was for only a few hours. In the two days a week that I was able to sneak away, I ran to the yoga studio. Yoga was the first thing I found that connected my mind, body, and spirit and I craved that alone time each week.

Always being an avid reader, I loved fueling my mind diving into personal development. And with a strong foundation in faith, I assumed I was covered there, too. But yoga? That combined all three things on a mat. I found myself looking forward to stretching my mind and body more and more each class. In a dark, 100-degree room, with two minutes of meditation at the end. It was torture, yet I craved it. I couldn't get enough. Every day that I showed up on my mat, I learned something different. No two classes are the same. You may follow the same sequence, the same flow, and yet only you dictate how it's going to go. Your body is tense. Your mind is on overdrive. Your stressed. Your angry or resentful or frustrated as hell. No matter how you show up on your mat, you meet yourself there. Present. You show up as yourself and leave a better version of yourself.

It was on the mat that I learned a very powerful lesson in my journey. I found myself running out the door to class after a long weekend of solo parenting. I needed alone time and to search for the same thing I had been searching for the past 17 years. Me. I was still stuck on the notion of how life should've been. I never expected that pain wasn't a part of the equation of life, but as a member of the Xennial generation, I was still raised to believe that if I worked hard enough and did everything in the right order, I would be *successful*. I identified with that notion and belief in *one day*.

Well, I found myself pissed. The same thoughts resurfaced. I had done everything in the right order. I had the fancy degrees. I had the jobs with the titles. I had the supportive husband and three great kids and a dog. I had it all. And yet, why wasn't I successful? I left those degrees and titles at the door when I decided to work for myself. I married a supportive husband who supports from afar because he's working his ass off to provide for our family. I was home and present for my boys except I resented it most days. This wasn't successful. This wasn't what I signed up for.

But that day on the mat, where I met my true self, I shifted. I realized that life is messy and beautiful and loud and exactly what I had always needed...not what I always envisioned. I met myself with where I was at instead of focusing on where I needed to be.

As time went on, I discovered what was really eating at me was finding myself back in the same complacent space I recognized as familiar. On the outside, it looked like I had it all. Three beautiful and healthy boys, a part-time job with my mentor where I worked from the comfort of my easy chair, and the time and flexibility in the world to get things done. Only on the inside, I was an uninspired hot mess.

I was booking more and more speaking events, yet there was a pull of inauthenticity. I was speaking on leadership and owning your story when I wasn't owning mine. I felt like a complete fraud. I was afraid of truly being seen. I continued to play small for fear of being viewed as the broken girl I was seen as at the age of fifteen.

Not trusting my own intuition, I became habitual seeking answers from others. After having such an intense connection to the Divine through Joy, I sought seekers and healers to share more from the spirit world. I required confirmation that I was on the right path. My addiction to control reared its ugly head and instead of being in flow, I became paralyzed and resisted any movement for fear of making the wrong step. Statistics of entrepreneurs failing plagued my thoughts and I couldn't possibly dare to misstep.

• • •

One night after I put the boys to bed, I waited excitedly for my phone to ring. I had booked a session with an intuitive who connected with angels. At 8:30 p.m. on the dot, my phone rang, and I answered having my notebook and pen ready. As she started, she asked a couple questions to start dialogue and to gauge where we were going in this session.

"Tell me where you're at and where you'd like to go," she said.

"I am so lost," I explained. "I have all these gifts, talents, and passions. Yet, I do not see how they all overlap. Am I speaker? Am I a writer? Am I supposed to be in sales? In my work now, I feel like I'm losing my own voice. I am not creating anything on my own when I'm a creative person. Then there's a part of me who wants to switch directions and go through yoga teacher training and travel the world teaching."

"Okay, and what is it that you'd like to know?" she asked.

"Which direction do I choose? Because right now I feel like I'm good at a lot of different things versus being great at a few," I said.

"Your focus is too wide," she started. "You're a dreamer, so that's why you see everything big picture. Everything that you're doing is right where it's meant to be."

Oh my God, not again. "I know this, but I'm so sick of hearing it," I confessed, clearly frustrated. "When will it be clear to me what I'm supposed to be doing?"

"Do you believe in Spirit Animals?" she asked.

"Yes, absolutely," I said, knowing that I have had many messages from animals who crossed my path. My brother Mark reveals himself to me as an eagle and leaves feathers for me to show me he's near.

"Okay, good. There is a grey owl who is with you on your journey now," she said. "Owls represent the all-seeing eye. Meaning, they can turn their heads almost 360 degrees to see everything. They watch their prey and wait until the exact moment to strike."

I smiled at the synchronicity of another bird spirit animal.

"Like the owl, you are watching and learning everything there is to be learned right now," she continued. "It's not time for you to strike. Everything leading up to this point has been filed for you to use in the future."

"That makes sense," I said. "It has been a big learning curve on all levels. I know God's timing is infinitely better than my own. I just hate being patient."

"I know. But trust that it's for the best," she said. "And like when an owl flies, it's breathtaking and people stop to watch their flight. That will be you. You'll know when to soar, and people will stop to witness it."

"Wow. Okay," I said taken aback. "That makes me feel better."

"And you said something about yoga?" she asked, which surprised me.

"Yeah, it's something I've been ruminating in the back of my mind," I confirmed. "There's a teacher training in Bali I've been looking at, but I'm not sure if that's my thing." Aaron already said no to teacher training, as it's not a money-making venture, I thought. But the thought of not having any responsibilities and traveling doing yoga instead of being in the fires of motherhood hell sounds pretty appealing.

"I see you there," she said, which caught me off guard. "You will meet someone there who will make a huge impact on your life. It will be a brief exchange, but the message you come home with will be transformational."

"Seriously?" I asked, flabbergasted at the detail she was describing.

"Yes," she confirmed. "If you have the chance, do it. Go."

chapter twelve

A NEW DAY

A s I retrieved my bag and started walking to exit the airport, the energy was magnetic, and I could hardly believe I had made it. Twenty-nine hours ago, I was leaving the tundra of Northern Minnesota and five plane changes later, I arrived in Bali.

A surge of pride bubbled up inside as I thought back to the tension between Aaron and I leading up to before I left. *And he didn't think I would make it. Hell, he didn't think I should even come.* It's true, the weeks leading up to my trip, Aaron became despondent towards me. Instead of asking about my trip, he sent me Google searches of what to be wary of and how to protect myself when traveling abroad. Even as he drove me to the airport, he didn't say two words until he parked in front of the Arrivals terminal to drop me off.

"Don't go," he whispered, grabbing my hand.

"What?!" I looked at him incredulously, completely aghast. "You're really going to do this now? My flight is in two hours. The entire trip is paid for! I'm not going to just eat that money!" *Oh hell no. I worked damn hard saving for this trip. The hell if I'm gonna let it go to waste.*

"It's not about the money. I just don't want you to go," he said softly. I saw a glimmer of sadness in his eyes.

"I need to do this, Mister," I reaffirmed. "You need to let me go and soar on my own." I smiled and squeezed his hand to reassured him even more. "Trust me."

And with a kiss goodbye, I was off.

The sweet and sticky air filled my lungs and I immediately knew I was overdressed in my layers of day old airplane clothes, but I was more engrossed in finding my ride.

I turned on my phone and connected to the Wi-Fi, looking for the email that had which driver was picking me up. "*The driver will have a sign with Surya Kempar on it, along with your names,*" read the directions. I scanned the crowd of drivers with all the names on their 8x11 paper, but none had my name or the name of our resort.

Panic tried to sink in. *Here we go again,* I thought, flashing back ten years ago pre-international cell phone plans, when the same thing happened to me in Spain. Only I didn't speak or read a lick of Spanish and I spent hours crying alone in the airport waiting for my college roommate, who was studying abroad at the time, to pick me up. *Not this time,* I calmed myself as I just breathed. *I made it all the way here, I'm not going to give up this early.*

I knew I was arriving on the same flight with three other people going to the same yoga retreat, but the kicker was that I didn't know who they were. I signed up for a yoga retreat with a group of complete strangers, knowing only one person, but even then, hadn't seen her in six years, in a foreign country halfway across the world and trusted that all would be okay. You only live once, right?

Just then I saw a lone, blonde-haired beauty with a yoga mat who was looking for her ride, but retreated back like I did waiting, so I took a chance.

"Excuse me, are you here for a yoga retreat?" I asked.

She looked up at me from her bag and smiled, "Why, yes I am!" *Success!* Relieved, I gushed, "Awesome! I can't find our resort name on a sign. Is that what you were looking for, too?"

The sweet girl looked very confused and said, "I didn't request a car ahead of time. I was looking for one right now."

Sheepishly, I asked, "Are you not here for the Soul Yoga Retreat in Ubud?"

I could see the pity in her face as she replied, "No, sorry. Wrong retreat."

I was so embarrassed. *Of course there is more than one yoga retreat going on right now,* I thought. *Ubud is the known for its retreats. This isn't small town Minnesota anymore, Kathryn.*

I checked the time on my phone again, trying to gain semblance on the 14-hour time difference from home. By now it had been at least 20 minutes since I first entered the pickup line, and close to 2 hours since our flight came in since Customs was a disaster to get through. *Maybe our driver left with the other group,* I thought. I walked down the long line of cabbies waiting for their guests to arrive to search for my name again.

"Amanda?" one cabbie asked as he smiled at me.

"No, Kathryn," I said.

"Where you going?" he asked back.

"Um, Sur-ee-ya Kem-bar?" I answered, but questioning my answer as my thick Minnesota accent reflected my mispronunciation of the resort.

"Kat-reen?" a voice called out behind all the cabbies. "Kat-reen?" And then I see a smiling face as he made his way through until he saw me. "Kat-reen! We've been waiting for you! Here, come!"

A flood of relief poured over me and I practically skipped through the airport with my purple bag to find the rest of the group waiting by the massive, arched open-air entrance to the airport.

"There she is! Hello!" a woman smiled and put her arm around me. "We were worried sick about you! We thought we lost you, but didn't know what you looked like, so we didn't know how to find you! We kept scouring social media, and yet none of them were you!"

I laughed as I began stripping layers of clothes off. The shock of being lost was wearing off and reality sinking in with the 90-degree temperature and 80% humidity difference from home. "I know, right? I figured I'd use my own advice I give my boys and stay right where I was supposed to be, and someone would find me!"

The rest of the group waiting introduced themselves and we grabbed our things and followed our drivers to the vehicles parked in the parking ramp across the street. It was my first glimpse of paradise as I walked out onto the street and looked up at the big, blue sky cradled by massive palm trees and exotic birds flying overhead. The sounds of horns honked and the throngs of people that passed us really gave it away that I was actually here. I silently squealed inside. *Eeek! I actually did this!*

• • •

The vans slowly drove into the driveway of our resort an hour later, and I was mixed with emotions. I was excited, yet in the pit of my stomach, I was petrified. *What have I done flying across the world? Will Roni even remember me? Will we pick up right where we left off? It's been six years since we last saw each other...right after James was born.* I let my mind wander and ramble, which quickly turned into a pep talk. *I mean, we practically lived together, and she was my nurse when I delivered James so of course it will be alright.* Trying to keep my composure together, *Stay open, Kathryn. You're meant to be here.*

When I was checking in, I heard a lot of excitement followed by hugs and checking how flights were and the usual travel to do. As I turned around, before me was the sweetest petite gal with bright eyes and charismatic energy that sucked me in before she even opened her mouth.

"Kathryn!" she smiled with arms opened wide. "I'm Yvette! Yay! I am so excited you're here!"

"Hi!" I answered with a hug. "I can't believe I am actually here!"

"Well, you gave us all a little scare as we thought we lost you," Yvette winked, still holding me by my arms. "And all I could think of is how we lost Roni's friend on the first day! But good news, we found you and you're here!"

"I'm here!" I replied with a laugh. I looked right past Yvette and saw my long-lost friend emerge from the staircase. My heart stopped, and instantaneous tears welled in my eyes as I brushed past the others to reach her.

"Roni," I breathed into her as I held her close. "Oh, Roni." I couldn't let go. She squeezed me back in the same bear hug as she used to give and whispered, "I am so glad you are here. I've been waiting for this for a long time."

She broke the hug, but still held onto me and stared deep into my eyes, "It's going to be magical. You just wait and see."

"I'm sure you guys need to move more, so let's get these kids to their room and settled. We'll all meet down at the shala for some restorative yoga at 5:30 am and have supper here tonight, followed by a little welcome after that," announced Yvette. "You guys, follow me," she said to the other group. "Roni, you take Kathryn to your suite."

I grabbed my bags and followed Roni through an open archway to a private pool and four rooms.

"We each have our own room," Roni said.

"What? I thought we were sharing a room?" I asked, confused, knowing I only paid for a double occupancy.

"Well Yvette thought this was a house with four rooms when she booked it," Roni explained. "Only, it's a suite with four separate rooms with king-sized beds and outdoor showers."

"Shut up," I said, in denial as I soaked in our private suite. *I'm officially in paradise*, I thought. The deep aqua blue water of the infinity pool was just steps out our front doors. A privacy fence was covered in thick, green, jungle plants and flowers. The chirping of insects and birds were hard to define yet soothing to the ear.

Roni walked me up to Suite D and opened the floor to ceiling glass doors and said, "Welcome home, babe." I stepped into the air conditioning and took note of the details in the room as I set my stuff down. The high, vaulted ceilings with the bamboo fan at the center, the teal ottoman which matched the water outside, and the large mosquito net that framed the bed. "Wait 'til you check out the bathroom," said Roni as opened a side door.

I walked through to the bathroom to find an oversized stone tub and outdoor shower. "Shut up," I said again, unable to comprehend this was my home for the next week.

"I know, right?" Roni squealed. "Come check out my room, it's a teeny bit different, and so is Kat's." We crossed the lanai and checked out her glorious room. All seemed to have different themes to them, all within a wooden, leafy, nature-esque realm contrasting the natural stone elements. Absolutely stunning and it solidified my notions of what Bali would look and feel like. Paradise. We finally made our way down to yoga and found ourselves in a circle all facing one another.

"Before we begin, we'll save and do the introductions and all that jazz after supper at the official welcome," Yvette started. "This is just a stretching practice to loosen up after all of you flew in today."

• • •

After supper, we all made our way to the other end of the resort property where the majority of the group was staying. While we ate, I started to gain a good understanding of who came with whom and how they were all interconnected. I sat down on the bench next to Roni and watched as everyone piled around the poolside in beach chairs in their comfy clothes, jetlagged from the flight and yet excited for what was unfolding for the week. Yvette found her spot right next to me and laid her head on my shoulder for a brief moment.

"As I created this retreat, I set out the intention that an intimate group is what was required," Yvette started out, looking at everyone around her. "This is the sixth retreat we've had, and already, I can tell that those of you who came are meant to be sitting here." She patted my leg intentionally and I smiled knowing that was the truth.

"So, as we embark on this week together, let's open ourselves to new experiences, new friendships, and new lessons to be set forth," she continued. "We are a family here, and many of us have been retreating together two, three, six times! So, just so you know, this is a family...an open, loving, come-as-you-are family, and we are so happy to open it up to new faces this year."

Yvette took my hand, smiled as she turned to me and said, "Why don't you start?"

I laughed and said, "Nothing like making the new kid go first, huh? Well, hi ya'll. I'm Kathryn and I'm from Minnesota. I know Roni from college as we are sorority sisters." I grabbed Roni's hand with my free hand and continued, "She actually helped deliver my first-born."

"It's true!" Roni piped in, referring to her work as an obstetrics nurse.

"I've actually stalked Yvette for the past few years on Instagram once I knew that it was Roni's friend who hosted all these amazing retreats I saw her going on," I continued. "When this popped up on my feed, I immediately texted Roni and sent in my deposit. No questions, just trusted that I needed to be here."

"You literally signed up for a retreat knowing absolutely no one," one guy pressed in awe.

"I sure did," I confirmed. "I left my three boys at home with my husband and I left. I have never been so sure that I needed to be here in my life."

"Wow," said Yvette. "I love that you took a chance on us...on me... and opened yourself up to a whole new experience. That's amazing!"

I beamed at how far I'd come. Literally and figuratively. Trusting myself. Trusting the pull of my soul and listening to it. Showing up for me. Sitting beside my old friend and making new ones. I was ready. One-by-one, the others introduced themselves, all from the Phoenix, Arizona area and had a major element in common: all of them were students of Yvette's. I was surprised to find that I was one of the youngest in this diverse co-ed group, as ages ranged from 30-60. Some couples, some came with their best friend, and some, like me, came alone to open themselves up to this new experience. However, witnessing the interactions and love that everyone shared, it cemented a bond that I was wholeheartedly ready to be a part of. I knew that this week was going to be life changing in more ways than one.

We bid goodnight for a restful night sleep. Only sleeping eight hours during a 29-hour travel day was starting to make me delirious, yet a mix of excitement and adrenaline was keeping me going. Noticing I missed the small window I had to FaceTime with the boys as they already left for school, I pulled out my trusty journal that became a lifeline to me after all of these years; documenting fears, dreams, aspirations, and explorations.

This is the start of something new, I started. *I am exactly where I am meant to be. I survived, and I am made for more. I am watching it unfold before my eyes.*

• • •

Turns out, just as the Universe would have it, the retreat proved to be everything I needed it to be. It wasn't a teacher training like I originally wanted, but yoga in Bali with no expectations or responsibilities. It's what I needed. We had yoga twice a day and each day was filled with either an excursion to waterfalls, sacred temples or different beaches where we would soak up as much of the Balinese culture that we could take. If we weren't at the resort, lunches and dinners consisted of the different fares of Bali. Farm to table, rice paddies, and traditional ethnic gourmet meals filled our bellies.

On the second night, however, after a grand day of hiking up a waterfall, we all sat family-style around the dinner table in the open-air restaurant at the resort. In front of us was a buffet of freshly caught fish, sautéed vegetables, home-cooked bread, and freshly picked fruit, garnished by exotic wildflowers that were picked just for us. I was getting out of my head and began feeling more versus thinking. I wanted to experience the entire experience and not be tied at the hip to Roni, so I made sure to sit next to others and learn more about them. This night, I found myself next to one of my suitemates, Kat.

"Oh my gosh, I love your mala," I said to her, trying to start a conversation during the meal. I instantly recognized the black onyx, but the gray and silver stones that accented the mala just caught my eye.

"Thanks!" she said as she rubbed her hand over it as it was wrapped beautifully around her wrist. "I just got this one, actually. I went in to get one of my other malas fixed and for some reason, this one just called out for me. So instead of bringing my other mala, I bought this new one for the trip to infuse Bali's goodness into the stones."

"That's awesome," I said. "We don't have much for stones and malas up where I'm from, so that's my goal while I'm here. I want to buy a mala as a keepsake from my trip. That would be so special to me."

"You don't have one?" Kat asked.

"Nope," I replied. "Do you wear yours all the time or meditate with it?"

"No, I don't typically wear jewelry, so this is my statement piece," Kat said. "Plus, I love and connect with crystals, so this is perfect for me."

"I love that," I said, still glancing at it from the corner of my eye as I ate.

"Do you miss your kids?" Kat asked, continuing on the conversation.

Well... I thought. "Yes and no," I admitted. "I mean I do, yet there's something about being halfway around the world away from them that gives me so much peace. I needed this. And they need their father and he is so amazing that they probably don't even realize I'm gone."

"I can understand that," she said. "It sounds like you had a full plate before you left."

Ha, more like the plate overflowed and eventually cracked under the weight of it all. "I did. I was so burned out emotionally from solo parenting and behavioral issues with the boys," I replied. "I booked this trip in the midst of the chaos. It was my beacon. Thankfully we are on the upswing of everything, but I was getting bogged down by so much, I was more than ready to get on that plane."

"I can only imagine!" answered Kat, with a kind smile.

"You were Roni's roommate?" I asked, already knowing the answer, yet trying to dive in deeper.

"Yes, we lived together for a number of years, and we even worked in the same OB unit in Phoenix," she replied. "We both moved and started work at the same time, so we did a lot of growing up together."

"Love that. Roni and I practically lived together," I said.

"Yes, I knew that," Kat said. "When we met, she said she had another Kat in her life from college! Did you know my name is Kathryn, too? Spelled the same way, even."

"Really? That's awesome," I mused. "You even have my old initials, KW."

"Well look at us," Kat beamed and grabbed my hand. "Twins. It's so amazing that you're here. That took a lot of courage to just show up."

"I was nervous," I admitted. "That feeling of 'oh crap what did I do' went through my mind the entire time, but I just trusted and look at the beautiful souls I am surrounding myself with."

Kat beamed. We instantly knew we had a connection. Little did I know how strong that would be.

• • •

Day after day, Kat and I found ourselves mighty inseparable. Between scouring the beaches for shells to running into the ocean hand and hand not to get swept up by the undercurrent to our late-night angel card readings, our souls were intertwined. I loved how easy it was to open up and just be me around everyone there, especially Kat. Truly, authentically me. No masks, no agendas. Just me.

On our fifth day on the island, our group visited a black sand beach close to our resort in Jaseri versus spending two hours in the car to get to the ocean. As we walked through the jungle on a sandy path, I was speechless to the exquisite beauty that surrounded us. I could hear the ocean, but it wasn't until we walked through the canopy boughs of lush, green leaves that I glanced at the magnificent beauty that laid before me. Glistening under the vibrant sun and clear blue sky was the most breathtaking black sand beach. It was so magnificent that each of us stopped to take it all in.

"Oh my God," I breathed out in awe. "I've never seen anything like this!"

Kat and Roni were right beside me, entranced. "Look at how the sand glistens more than the ocean!" Roni said. "This just keeps getting more and more incredible!" She pointed to the left, "Look, there are all the surfers!" Jaseri Beach was known for their big waves and incredible surfing.

"Let's run in," Kat gushed, a sucker for running into the waves. We all hurried to the edge of the beach, dropped our things and ran towards the water.

We all squealed as we ran, not anticipating the scorching element that black sand does to the soles of your feet. The cool rush of the ocean waves gave immediate relief to our poor feet. "Next time wear shoes up until the water," we mused after learning our lesson. We splashed around for a bit, watched some of the surfers from afar, and decided to head back to the bar and pool where everyone else was at ordering food and drinks. Pool floaties, watermelon sangria, and appetizers filled the rest of our afternoon. The mermaid that I am, I barely got out of the water. Others took naps, read books, saddled up to the bar, but Kat and I lounged in the sun on our floaties talking about life.

"Have you found your mala, yet?" Kat asked.

"Nope. Nothing feels right," I replied. "I know what I'm looking for, but I don't want to buy one just to buy one. I'm hopeful when we go shopping at the market tomorrow I'll find it. Or it will find me."

"Right. Actually, it feels as if we were meant to find each other," Kat confessed. "On this trip, you know? I almost didn't come for fear of what would surface, like some previous retreats I've been on. But I think the reason I came was, so I could meet you."

My soul leaped. "I totally know what you mean," I gushed right back, feeling that deep connection. "It's like our souls just knew. I mean, I knew this would be a life changing trip. What I didn't expect is to find a soul sister."

It wasn't the sun, it wasn't the sangria. It was our souls that were doing the talking. An undeniable, kindred spirit that connected us. As if we were sisters in another lifetime, catching up on current events. I was amazed at how our lives ran parallel to each other, even though we had so many opposites. Both of us had the same initials, two older brothers, same sandy-colored hair and blue-green eyes, same long and lean stature, entrepreneurial goals instead of working corporate jobs, and romantics at heart. I recognized myself in her, only two steps ahead. I was able to share insight and wisdom that I learned on my journey as she was going through it presently.

Out of the corner of my eye, I saw Roni, who just finished her book, floating at arms-length away and came to join us. She was watching us from afar and overheard our conversation.

"I love watching how you two get lost in each other," she said with a smile. "It's literally been one of the highlights of this trip."

"Aww," I said back with a smile. "That makes my heart smile. We were just saying that we think the reason why we came on this trip was so that we could find each other."

"I know the reason why I came on this trip," she said with a smile. "It was to bring you two together."

Kat and I looked at each other with wide grins.

"It's so clear to me now," said Roni, joining our hands together. "I'm a connector. I bring people together. It's fate and the Universe that we are all here together. We're a triangle; impossible to break." And with that last word, she squeezed our hands tight, emphasizing our now sacred bond.

••••

As I got further into the week, I felt as though something was missing. Even though Yvette had these amazing excursions and experiences planned out for us, there was still something tugging; a pull from my soul.

I'd always been called to the mountains. For someone who lived smack dab in the prairie, the thought of climbing up towards heaven and to see the majesties of God's land from a whole new view was amazing. In Bali, they had guided sunrise hikes up their two mountains. The catch was, you have to be on the top to watch the sun actually rise. Which presumably means, you have to hike in the middle of the night. That didn't make me waver; I knew I needed to go. It was after our epic black sand excursion that I asked Kat if she wanted to go hiking with me.

"I'm being called to the mountains," I admitted at our supper that night.

"The mountains?" Kat confirmed as she took a sip of wine. "What mountains?"

"There is a sunrise hike up Mt. Batur," I explained. "And I want to hike it."

"How long is it?" Kat asked, obviously piquing interest.

"I believe it's like between two and two-and-a-half," I shared nervously, for fear that'd scare her.

"Total or like five hours round trip?" she asked.

"Five hours round trip," I confirmed. "And you'd have to hike in the dark, but they say it's totally worth it to see the sun rise."

"I'll go," Kat said without hesitation. The shock on my face must have led her to elaborate. "I love hiking, I actually do it quite a lot at home."

"Really?" I said, blown away that she didn't even have to think twice, as I was weighing this on my mind for weeks.

"Yeah, I'm in. I just hiked up Camelback last weekend before

I left, and that's a seven hour hike," she smiled. "I say let's go."

Those around us heard our conversation, and we opened it up to the entire group, but hiking in the middle of the night didn't seem to intrigue the rest of the group like it did for us.

"I guess it's just you and me," I said holding up my glass to Kat.

"I wouldn't have it any other way," she replied, toasting me back.

• • •

Not knowing what to expect, we could hardly sleep that night. We had a 2 a.m. alarm set, and we stayed up until 12:30 a.m. in sheer excitement talking. We were out front of the resort as our tour bus arrived by 3 a.m. to start our journey. Before we knew it, we had our flashlights in hand and followed our tour guides to the base of the mountain.

"Are you ready for this?" Kat asked me.

"More than ready," I replied, trying to mask my nerves. She was an avid hiker, so this was right up her alley. I was going more on a soul journey than physical activity.

It was 4 a.m. It was pitch black with nothing to guide us besides the full moon looming and the glow of our flashlights. It was an estimated two hour hike up the mountain, with a few spots to rest. I looked up the mountain and saw the trail of flashlights moving. *I feel you, God*, I thought, setting the intention as I started the ascent, *I trust you. I am open to whatever lessons are to come from this experience.*

We followed the path as it got closer and closer to the foot of the mountain, where it got narrower and narrower until it became a single path. As much as I wanted to look around and see where we were going or those around me, I could only look at one step in front of me, as it was so dark, and the trail was even more rugged. Loose rock, large steps, and not much light led for immense focus and concentration.

About an hour in, we stopped for a couple minute break and we saw other groups passing us. "How many people are hiking today?" I asked one of our guides, as we were all huddled together.

"Around three-hundred people hike each morning," he replied in his broken English.

"All on this little trail?" I mused to Kat. "There's not much room to stop on the side of a mountain."

"No, not at all," she replied. "You doing okay?"

"Yeah, I am," I said. "The anticipation is mounting as we keep going. I can't even explain it, but I feel it."

"I know," Kat said, smiling. I caught a twinkle in her eye when she said, "I feel it, too."

Before we knew it, we were back on our way. We made friends with the gal hiking behind us, as she seemed to be hiking solo. Turns out, she was from China, on her spring break and decided to book a trip on her own since she had five days off. Hiking Mt. Batur was on her bucket list, so here she was. *A girl not afraid to go after it*, I mused. *I love that.*

By the time we made it to the first summit, we could see a thin line of light illumniating on the horizon. It was still dark, but we could make out the second mountain across the way and the cloud coverage over the ocean.

"How much longer to the top?" someone asked our guide.

"Twenty minutes," he replied. "We make good time."

I saw the trail of lights from other hikers moving to the top and I turned to Kat, "I want to keep going. All these breaks are making me antsy...especially since we can see the top!"

"You ready?" our guide asked me.

"Yes! Let's go!" I said excitedly.

"This part rocky," he warned all of us. "It go up and up. No place to stop. Watch your foot." He was right. It was steep and filled with very small crevices for footings as you made your way up. As we climbed, I started feeling the previous two hours of hiking in my legs, but I continued to push through. Nothing was going to stop me from seeing this sunrise. Once we made it to the top, others who already made it there, cheered. *Now this is my kind of welcome*, I thought.

"We go over here with other guides," our guide told us. "You stay here. We will get you when time to go." Kat and I looked around the throngs of people and weaved our way to the edge to look around.

"Can you believe this?" I breathed out as I soaked in the breathtaking view lighting up before us.

"This is amazing," she replied back, clearly in awe.

"Let's go down there on the side of the mountain and find a spot," I pointed further down where we saw a few others camping out waiting for the sun to fully rise. "It doesn't look nearly as crowded."

We cropped a spot in a little grassy knoll that fit just the two of us. We pulled out our second breakfast: the Styrofoam container of hard boiled eggs and toast they sent us up the mountain with and that we heard creak in our backpacks on the way up. Armed with our phones, we were ready to witness God's beauty. What we weren't ready for was the immense energy that surged within us as the sun rose.

I was overcome with emotion as I saw and felt the power of sun fill me. Tears filled my eyes and my soul leaped. It was like I was having another out of body experience, as my soul took over. My body stood up and with open arms I filled my entire being with the light of the sun, penetrating each nook and cranny of my body, heart, and soul. Although it was chilly at the top, I let the sun's warmth wash over me and fill me from the inside out.

Feeling the surge of energy within me, I felt Kat's hand find mine and I lost it. There we were, linked hand in hand, soaking in one of the greatest moments of my life, with tears rolling down our faces; releasing any darkness that remained within us.

I let the light of the sun reflect my entire being. I was it and it was me. I know there were other people on that mountain, but in those moments, it was only Kat and I as we were alone within the Universe. Energy flowing within us and through us. We were one. God was within us. It was beyond electrifying and yet indescribable.

As our senses finally came back and we intentionally grounded ourselves back into the world around us, we wiped our tears and as any yogi would do, we ended our epic session with honoring the sun with Sun Salutations, which are heart chakra openers. As if we needed any more, but it felt good to move that energy out throughout us.

"Wow, I can't believe this," I said as I started cleaning up our spot. "So powerful, right?"

Before we moved off the side of the mountain, Kat said, "Hang on, I've got something for you. Close your eyes."

"What?" I asked, genuinely confused.

"Just close your eyes," she directed, and I obliged.

I felt her touch my hand and place something in it, yet she cupped my hands to keep them closed. Instinctively I knew exactly what it was and gasped as the beads pulsated in my hand.

"Now open them," I could hear her say with a smile.

I opened my eyes and hands to see Kat's beautiful face with the sunrise behind her and her beautiful mala in my hands. My eyes filled with tears and I tried to ask questions, but no words came out.

"I was hoping you wouldn't find your mala this week," she started to explain with tears welling in her own eyes and still cupping my hands. "When someone comments on a mala, it means that it calls out to them. It's meant for that person. That's why it called me before I left on this trip, it knew I would find you."

"I can't take this," I said in utter disbelief. "This is yours."

"No, it's not," Kat smiled. "It's been yours the entire time, but I didn't want to sound like a crazy person and give it to you the second day without you even knowing me." She laughed. "I wore it every day on all of our excursions so that it has all of our adventures fused into those stones. So now you have me and Bali to take home with you."

The crystals of the mala were warming my hand, as if to tell me it was home. I squeezed my hand over them and embraced Kat in a soul-filling hug. "I love you," I whispered into her ear as I held her tight. "You have filled a spot in my heart that I didn't know was missing. You are forever my soul sister."

"I know," she whispered back through the tears. "And you are mine."

After we broke our embrace, we loaded up on pictures, found the rest of our group and began the descent down the mountain. It was surprisingly harder going down than up, as there were no rails to help, and loose rock freely fell down the hill. We stopped to see the volcano's crater and to feel the steam from the magma under our feet.

In the moment, I couldn't feel anything else besides sheer awe and appreciation for what just unfolded. The magic of my kindred spirit being strengthened through the sunrise. I knew that surge of sunlight shot through my soul and cracked open a new part of me. I didn't realize it at the time, but I transformed on the side of that mountain. I was ready to mirror that light into the world.

"You have seen my descent.
Now watch my rising..."

– Rumi

chapter thirteen

....

NEW GROWTH FROM OLD ROOTS

B y the time I landed back in Minnesota after a life-changing ten days, I was anxiously waiting for three sets of little arms to be wrapped around my neck. The frigid air of only 15 degrees didn't faze me as I stood outside finally breathing the familiar crisp air that welcomed me home. When I saw the black Chevy Tahoe pull up, my soul leapt again, only for a different reason. I recognized the dark and handsome face driving, smiling with relief to see me standing on the snow-scattered sidewalk.

I opened the car door with tears brimming, as I was welcomed with screams and cheers that made my heart sing. I scrambled to get in and felt at peace being back with my people again. For every adventure I go on, my soul feels at home with the souls that are my four boys. My entire world right in front of me.

"Hey guys!" I exclaimed, smiling from ear to ear, leaning into the backseat for fluffy winter jacket hugs, squeezing through the padding to feel their little hearts beat next to mine. "Oh, my goodness, how did you grow so big while I was gone?" The chatter that ensued about their adventure with Daddy filled the vehicle. I looked over at Aaron, and my heart burst with pride to see him beaming. I leaned in for a kiss and hug.

"Hi, Mister," I said. "I missed you." His heartfelt smile said it all. I knew he was more than happy to have his whole heart back, too.

The hour-long ride home was eventful as I heard all about the weeklong adventure the boys had with Aaron. They tattled on all the treats they ate, who had more time-outs than the other, and that they were only late for school one day.

"How many times did you order pizza for supper?" I asked winking at Aaron, half kidding, but I knew Aaron and his preplanning skills. "Three times!" James offered easily. Aaron laughed and tried to justify, but the giggles from the backseat drowned out his explanation.

As we pulled into the drive, that red rambler never looked so good. When I left just ten short days earlier, I resented that house. I felt trapped inside of it; working from home and raising three boys as a solo parent while Aaron worked on the road. I viewed it as a silent cage that I placed myself in, a dream that I created into reality. To work from home to create a schedule and life that I so desired; not realizing the shadow of that is always being on, always being needed, and not able to escape.

But now it looked different. Now it looked so peaceful surrounded by the fresh blanket of snow that had fallen the night before. A serene sight as the sun set fading behind the trees in the background. The same sun that I watched rise over mountains across the world just two days earlier.

Or maybe, it was me who was different.

• • •

"Well, how was it?" Aaron finally asked after we settled on the couch together after we tag-teamed putting the boys to bed. "Tell me everything." We had FaceTimed many times on the trip, but it was more to see the boys and check in, not for in depth conversation. Plus with the 14-hour time difference, it made for quick five minute conversations before school or right at bedtime.

I started at the beginning. "You know how you didn't want me to get on the plane?" I asked rhetorically. "I know you were scared. But I had never been so sure of anything in my life. I was not scared. It's like my soul knew I needed this. Not to just get a reprieve from the mundane and ordinary like I thought I needed. It was more than that. It was like my soul needed to be reawakened to start taking action."

I knew part of that was true. Aaron didn't realize it, but subconsciously he was trying to keep me small. It made him uncomfortable to watch me grow and learn to fly on my own, and the only thing he knew to do was to ask me to stay. Yet deep down, he also knew he needed to let me soar. It was on the long trek back to the U.S. that I was able to reflect on how Aaron has always been my rock, my foundation to seek refuge in between the long journeys. I found peace understanding that God made him for me, strategically placed him in my life all those years ago. That no matter how far I go, Aaron will always be the one I can always come home to.

Aaron just sat listening, our legs intertwined as we sat facing each other, keeping his eyes intently on me as I continued. "Seriously, Mister. It was unlike anything I had experienced before. I opened myself up to new experiences, new people, and I just *trusted*. I let go of any preconceived notions of what I was supposed to do or who I was supposed to be, and I just showed up."

And that truly was the truth. I finally stripped off all the masks I had hid under, and I believe that's partly why I was so nervous to reconnect with Roni. She had known me in college as someone who was desperately trying to find herself but was losing herself in a downward spiral. The Kathryn that got off the plane in Bali was the real Kathryn, stripped down and authentic.

"The people I met were incredible," I continued. "Our group was so cohesive and we all meshed, there was no drama and no need for it. The yoga was incredible. Yvette was an amazing instructor and I learned so much in our short time together than I have in the year and a half I've been going to yoga here. We had the resort to ourselves practically, and the staff and our drivers treated us like family. The yoga shala was encapsulated by thick green shrubs and bushes, and sat next to a little creek, so every day we meditated with the sounds of water and birds. It was like my senses were on overload and I was in the middle of paradise. I keep saying this, but truly, it was paradise."

"It was so good to reconnect with Roni," I gushed. "It's like a piece of my heart from my past reconnected. But even more than that, I met the most amazing person, Kat. Mister, I'm serious when I say that we are kindred spirits reuniting. She was who I was texting in the car, saying I made it home safe." I went on to describe in detail the hike on Mt. Batur and the experience we shared together. I held up my wrist to show the mala wrapped around it. "Feel this," I said. "It has been warm and almost vibrating with energy since I put it on."

He wrapped his large, oversized hand around my petite wrist, and we both felt an electric current reverberate. "Huh," he said with surprised, wide eyes, not realizing that something so small could be so powerful. He let go of my wrist, instead moving it to my arm to keep close contact. "What was it like being there?" he asked, wanting to know more.

"The food was incredible. Everything was so fresh; harvested that day, so every day was different based on what was ready," I explained, grabbing my phone to show pictures as I talked. "Yvette tried hard to give us a full experience of the country, so each day we either ate or visited different parts of the country. Climbing the waterfall was incredible, as I had never imagined something that large or powerful. We climbed through rice paddies and by the time we got through the other side, I looked down and got pretty disorientated, so I opted to get the hell out before I either puked or rolled down to the bottom of the rice paddy. We visited three sacred temples and I swear to you, I felt it more than I saw it," I tried to explain, since pictures didn't do justice. "I mean, this temple is from the 11th Century, so it's just rocks and stones and statues, but the energy of sacredness was incredible. It was powerful."

"Mmmhmm," Aaron murmured as he flipped through the pictures. I could tell he was trying to soak in what I was saying and understand, but not fully grasping the gravity of it like I had being there. I stopped him at a certain point to explain the picture.

"This was taken at the water temple, and aside from the sun rise climb up Mt. Batur, this is probably my second favorite experience from Bali," I explained. "At each temple, it is required that you wear a sarong out of respect. Everyone wears one and even the men have to wear a head wrap," as I pointed out to our drivers who became our dear friends as they escorted us to each temple and explained their traditions.

"At the water temple, we participated in a purification ceremony, which was crazy powerful. It contains two pools with thirty showers of holy spring water, with each shower signifying a different cleanse," I explained, getting animated with my description. "At each shower, you bow for respect, splash your face three times and then fully immerse your head in the shower."

It was recommended that you go into the ceremony with a clear intention. I could feel the powerful energy of the sacred water along with the holy tradition and the collective energy of those around me. My intention was simple. It was to clear what no longer serves me. As I stood in front of each shower, I prayed, *Cleanse me. Heal me. Use me.* At the time, I did not realize how significant that prayer would become.

We continued to flip through pictures of food and gleaming beaches and smiling faces until we came to the end.

"You look happy," Aaron said finally.

"I am happy," I responded back.

"No, like different," he tried to explain, but at a loss as to how to word it. "I can tell there's something different."

I smiled and snuggled into him now that I was done recounting all the excitement and details of the past ten days. "This trip changed me," I said. "It opened a whole new part of me that I had been searching and searching for in all my therapy, books, and online courses."

I felt his heartbeat sync into mine as we lay holding each other close. "I can tell you're happy," he said.

"I am," I responded. "I truly am."

• • •

A few days later, my mom made a special trip to town for coffee while the boys were at school.

As we sat in our regular booth at the coffee shop—the one where she told me her tumor grew back—we sipped our coffee and munched on the peanut butter cookie we shared. I had just unloaded my Bali experience in a more practical manner for her, accompanied with scrolling through my camera roll for pictures. Her face lit up as we went through picture after picture of the ocean and beaches to the lush greenery outside my poolside room to the sunrise on the side of the mountain to crowded streets of the market.

"I am so proud of you for going," she finally said as I put my camera away and took another drink of my coffee. "Really, I am."

"Me, too," I responded. "I didn't know how much I needed it until I went."

"More than that," she said. "Yes, you needed to get a break

from doing everything on your own for so long. And those boys needed their father something fierce." She looked at me with tears welling in her eyes and continued, "I'm just so proud of who you're becoming. You've always had this fierce independence that I could never tame, and yet, something I've always wanted. You, my deary, are everything I have prayed for. And I am beyond blessed to witness you step into it."

Slightly taken aback at her words, yet finally feeling that strong connection to my mom again, I finally saw her for who she truly is. A resilient and proud woman who had always tried to give me more than she ever had, and in this moment, we both realized she actually did.

I leaned across the table and wrapped my hand gently around hers and tearfully squeezed it as I looked her in the eye and said, "I am who I am because of you."

• • •

My meditation practice intensified once I got back from my trip. Since I started on the journey of healing and transformation three years prior, I had been searching for answers and ah-ha moments in books, online courses, and through a series of life coaches after therapy with Joy. I dug into as much as I could, finding different gurus who would enlighten me along my path as I rediscovered myself. Gurus and experts who I put on a pedestal and hung on every word; believing that they would help me uncover myself. However, as I peeled off each mask and got closer and closer to my true self, I witnessed many of those gurus falling from my grace. Showing that they were, in fact, human...just like me.

It wasn't until I showed up as myself in Bali on the first day and stood on the side of the mountain with the sun pouring its light and energy into and throughout my entire being on the last day that I realized I didn't need to be looking externally anymore.

Everything that I needed to know, everything that I sought answers to I already had within me. Meditation was the practice that truly instilled that. I had meditated on and off for years, I realized. For meditation is simply focusing in on one's breath. In and out. Repeat. I remember doing this as a kid while I sat in my tree. I remember calming my mind in the drunk tank this to drown out the screaming and the shame that filled my thoughts. I remember bringing three little loves into the world by simply breathing.

As I made it a habit to focus my mind and sink into the stillness, I was amazed at how fast time would pass, how colors became vibrant, and how magnetic my energy would flow. I was so used to pleading to God for an answer, that I never realized that I needed to be quiet in order to hear His response. I didn't have to be reactionary in my responses anymore. If I sat and listened, I could co-create my responses, in line with God's purpose.

In addition to a meditation practice, yoga and journaling became daily practices too. In the midst of the chaos that most of the days ensued with raising three boys under the age of six, making time for myself was essential. There were days that I only got one of the three accomplished, and other days in which I hit the jackpot, I got all three done. I found that by taking this little slice of the day for myself, I reconnected to my soul, moved my energy purposefully, and recommitted to seeking answers within myself instead of from others.

I also found my tribe of powerful women to surround myself with locally. I missed that connection once I left Bali and Roni and Kat, and although we still connect via text and FaceTime, there's something about finding your tribe face to face. Each month the four of us connect over tea or green smoothies and share openly about motherhood, spirituality, yoga, entrepreneurship, and serving ourselves as a trinity: mind, body, and spirit.

One bright and sunny summer day, we met outside to soak in the warm sun with a light breeze, which is the quintessential perfect Northern Minnesota day. We found ourselves discussing manifesting, visualization, co-creating, and everything in between. All four of us are entrepreneurs and mamas with a background in radical self-compassion, so we all have goals of serving the world with our gifts and to demonstrate to our kiddos to do the same.

"I actually had a really epic meditation the other day," I confessed as I put my green smoothie down. We were sitting at a picnic table on the greenway and each of us had kicked our sandals off to opt for bare feet in the grass. "I was standing on a stage in front of like, two-thousand people, and I was holding my book," I said. "Then I saw my name in lights on the marquee outside of the stage that I was speaking on. It was so surreal, watching myself speak and hold a book of my life," I continued. "I saw women in the audience with tears running down their face; not out of pity or sorrow, but of feeling connected to my story and how it reflected in their lives. Almost as if they knew they were destined for more in life than they allowed themselves to be."

"Wow, that's powerful," said Jill, brushing the hair out of her face, knocking her sunglasses wonky on her face. She laughed, "How did it make you feel?"

"It was so real," I explained. "I saw it so clearly. I couldn't hear anything, but I knew what I was saying. Does that make sense?"

"Totally," they replied.

"I don't know, but it makes me feel so empowered. Like, confirmation that I'm on the right path that the best next thing is right around the corner."

"Oh, come on! You're rocking it as a writer already," said Becca, exaggerating with her arms. "You've been published by online journals. You're being featured in an upcoming book series. You have an inspirational journal coming up. It's about time that you tell your story."

My sunglasses hid the tears that were brimming my eyes as I realized at how much I had accomplished in just the past year alone, let alone what a journey this has been all together. What a stark contrast from the old Kathryn who continually questioned each step and didn't have vision farther than she could see. This Kathryn, the one sitting barefoot drinking a smoothie, talking to her tribe of independent, soulful women; this was a lit up and purposeful woman showing up in the world.

• • •

A few months later in September, I found myself seated at a table, anxiously checking and rechecking the time. *Ten more minutes until she takes the stage*, I thought. Others around me were taking their seats and I could feel the room's excitement. I noticed my energy was jittery. Half of it was from all the coffee I drank as I was on the road by 4 a.m. to drive four hours to meet one of my favorite authors in person, Glennon Doyle. The other half of it was from being on a high and actually meeting and hugging her as she signed my book just an hour beforehand. She was set to be the keynote speaker and I had just finished rereading her book, *Love Warrior*, for the third time the night before.

I had followed Glennon from her beginning as her blog caught notoriety and before she published her books. I was a young mom at the time and I fell in love with her brutal honesty of being real and raw. She didn't hide behind masks like I was at the time, and I admired her authenticity, integrity, and despite all the heartache that one can endure, show up as you are for the world.

During her talk, I listened intently in the audience. Between the belly laughs and tear-filled smiles, I couldn't help but beam and think of how far she has come. That by being a "shameless truthteller" as she called it, she has inspired millions of women to show up and be their authentic self too. Me included. Although many of the stories and lessons she shared during her keynote I had read or watched her speak about before, I still found myself taking notes. Antidotes and lessons that resonated on a whole new level, as if it were brand new information being downloaded in my brain.

"Pain is like a fire. It consumes you. But instead of running from the pain, you need to run *into* the pain," Glennon intently said from the stage. "Because if you are a person who has lived through so many fires that you know you are fireproof...that's when you know you're free."

Even in a room surrounded by 400 other women, I dropped my pen and just sat there as if Glennon specifically singled me out to tell me. I had been running from my past for so long that I dodged each and every fire. Instead I tried to outrun the wildfire that was consuming me. I wasn't free. I was suffocating. It wasn't until I did the work and healed my pasts, one-by-one, that I became the wildfire.

• • •

It's fall of 2017 and I find myself back at my childhood home, taking the familiar shortcut to the woods around the evergreen trees. I am not sure what to expect; it has been nearly 20 years since I have last traipsed through the woods surrounding the coulee. *Will I remember which tree it is? Will I know it once I see it? What if I don't find it? What if it doesn't live up to the enormity of what I saw as a child? Now coming as an adult, will it have the same energy it once had?* My thoughts race for what was to come. The mature corn stalks sway in the breeze as I follow the crop rows that winded around the coulee bends. When I see the familiar clearing, I step out of the field and into the long grass, unsure of what to expect.

Before I enter, I say a little prayer. *Show me what I need to know. Reveal yourself to me and teach me what I need to know.* Then I proceed into the thicket. A lot has overgrown in the past 20 years. Little trails that were once my prayer paths are lost. Landmarks that I once recognized as a child have fallen. New life grows on the wood bed, yet old broad trees still remain, only now as water-filled logs acting as balance beams across the coulee.

Yet the familiar draw to these woods I knew as a child still remains. Big and majestic in size, yet close enough that I can always find my way back. The way the sunlight flickers through the tops of the trees. The crunch of the yellowed leaves and moss-covered tree limbs under my boots. The smell of autumn that filled my body with every breath. It feels like home.

I creep through the brush and the thicket, picking up cockleburs as I go along. I notice animal tracks in the mud and berries that are freshly eaten off of bushes. At the base of the coulee, there are spots with water still standing, so I make my way to a thick, fallen tree to teeter across. As I do, I noticed how quickly my child-like agility and balance come back.

The deeper I walk into the woods, the more I start to doubt myself. *How will I ever find it again? Everything seems so broken. I'm guessing as to which direction it was.* Frustrated, I stop. I looked around and a calm comes over me. Two small black and white birds sing to me from a tree right above. I watch them play and carry on with one another until I silently ask them, *Show me where I need to be.*

They fly forward, and I take that as my cue to keep going. I follow the coulee and zig-zag back and forth between uprooted trees, broken branches, and spindly new tree growth. Two times I think I've found my tree, yet I don't get the intuitive feeling when I think I've come to the right one. Nothing looks the same, nothing feels the same. Instead, I feel defeated.

I decide enough is enough and I am going to walk back and

try a different route into the woods. I am too disorientated at not being able to follow the exact route I used to trod. The coulee itself has too much water to walk through and the edges are brimmed with brush and fallen tree debris to actually see big, massive trees.

As I crossed the coulee one more time, something out of the corner of my eye catches my attention. There is a clearing where a huge branch sits on the ground and I gingerly stand on it and walk to the base of the tree. *Could it be?* I think. I stop and hold onto a second tree and feel its power reverberate under my hand.

Instantly, I know. *Here she is.* I inhale a long breath and hold it for a moment, soaking it all in. As I exhale, I look down to the tree I am standing on and see how uprooted it was, fallen completely onto its side. I am now standing on one of the big boughs that I used to sit on as a child and dream. I step off and sit down, cherishing the same act that I did almost twenty years before. Moss has started to cover parts of its bark. Woodpeckers have made unique carvings out of it. It looks as if a fox has made a little den out of the base where a limb initially broke off and left an exposed hiding spot.

I trace my hands over the hearty knots and holes that remain on her trunk, now horizontal. The same knots and holes I remembered using as foot holes as I climbed. I stand up to look at the trees that grew around this massive fallen oak, only to realize that isn't the case. What I think is a single tree shooting up into the sky is in fact was a new bough sprouting from the old. I look at the other trees surrounding this one and sure enough, those are branches of this mighty oak, too.

New growth from old roots. How fitting.

This tree has withstood the storm. It bent. It broke. But its roots still run deep. It housed life for others. Some tried to break it down. But its roots run deep. It converged into other trees, entangling branches and limbs. New life is growing. It's still moving.

Bends, knobs, and holes. Molding. Growing and letting go. Her exterior may seem hard and brittle, neglected almost. Yet inside, she is still strong. Still whole, still full of life.

I feel her energy. I have come so far. And sitting in those branches I feel the same connection I had all those years ago. I think of Mark and how he is still a part of me, just as this tree always has been; watching and holding space.

I got lost, I got disorientated, I didn't know where I was. Looking around I couldn't see. And then I found you. Always calling me back home.

As I sit there watching the canopies of the old oak trees sway in the breeze and hearing the coulee babble, I revel in the fact of how still and simple life can be. We're the ones that continue to make it complicated. But when we're able to slow down and be still, even when it's uncomfortable or it hurts, we always make it to the other side.

Time and time again, my past has shown me that I will emerge on the other side stronger and more resilient. Now is the time to use that flame for good; to light up the world. But what I have come to realize is that I am beyond fireproof. Because even when the fire is smoldering, there is still smoke and ashes; remnants of what used to be.

No, I am a Phoenix. A symbol of transformation, rebirth, and resilience.

Like the sun each day, I reemerge new. Reborn from the ashes of my past. Ready to rise.

See yourself for who you are; right here, right now. It's hard. It's painful. But it's necessary. It's okay not to feel okay. To feel pissed, hurt, burned, and broken. But it's essential to reflect on your own lessons and meet yourself where you're at in the present moment. That's when you find your resiliency. To me, resiliency is a coming back to self.

I have already walked through the fires of hell and back, three times over. I've felt the heat. I was burned time and time again. I cried out for someone to put out the flame, only to find they were fanning them instead. I couldn't understand why this was still happening to me; I didn't deserve this. The shit that I no longer needed burned off; the relationships, people, situations, everything. Burned away. It hurt like hell and no, it wasn't pleasant. Until one day, when the fires were at their hottest, I realized something:

I am still here. I am still whole.

I am still resilient from the seasons that I weathered. The bending. The breaking.

I am still growing new life, new faith, and am rooted deeply in love. Still rooted in my trusting, in my hopes and in my dreams. The wisdom and guidance of that magical tree showed me I can do that.

I am still growing wild.

*"As the legend goes,
when the Phoenix resurrects
from the flames, she is even
more beautiful than before."*

- Danielle LaPorte

AFTERTHOUGHT

....

For most of my life, I was the master of shapeshifting. I placed all of my time and energy seeking for external validation because I was so lost. I lost who I was when I lost my innocence and my whole world shattered; much like the windshield I broke and flew through at the age fifteen. I tried picking up the pieces, and yet no matter how hard I tried, I couldn't piece them back together. Too many shards and cracks to find, let alone piece back together.

I had tried so hard to run away or create a new identity. I did not want to be the girl from the accident, I ran for almost two decades, only to look down and realize that I was the one who chained myself to that identity. Life a cuff hanging off of my leg, it went with me wherever I went; every new role or mask I placed on pretending that I let go of the past, there it was still hanging on. My accident became my crux. My excuse. My outer shell that I identified myself as... the one that kept me from doing and being everything I knew that I was.

People ask me all the time what I've gained from my journey. I can't give them one answer, because I've learned so much on my path. So, I always offer several.

Here are a few of the lessons I've learned:

I called myself home through forgiveness and acceptance. My breakthrough moment was in therapy when I finally forgave myself for searching for myself all these years. I lived an entire lifetime of seeking external results and archetypes of how to participate in the world; none of which were my truest self of identity. It was in the surrender of control that I finally saw myself for who I was. For the first time since I was a little girl, I feel whole.

I finally accepted my past. When I was able to understand and forgive that 15-year-old girl who was broken inside and out. Or the 23-year-old who found herself handcuffed in the back of the police cruiser and inside of the drunk tank. Or the 26-year-old new mom who had no idea how to raise a baby yet give him the world when she knew she couldn't. Or the 29-year-old lost daughter, caught between creating a life within and saving the one who gave her life. I wanted to understand who I was back then and embrace that girl. To tell her that she is stronger that she knows, wiser beyond her years, and that these lessons are only shaping her to teach and serve others. That it's okay not to feel okay, but one day, she will see the truth and light behind all of the tears. Just like the sun always rises, so will she.

I grieved the old life I thought I needed. The white picket fence around my newly remodeled house and a luxury SUV in the drive. Family meals every night, weekends at the lake, and family vacations at the beach. A thriving career, happy marriage, and balanced, well-rounded children. Picturesque. Social media-worthy. I already lived the shit life, I deserved the happily ever after. I worked my ass off. I checked all the boxes. I did it in the right order. And yet, I hadn't made it. I wasn't "there", wherever that was supposed to be. Instead, all of that brought more shame that I wasn't enough. Once I let go of the life I thought I needed to be happy, I realized I was already living a life that was pretty perfect for me. Three beautiful boys who adore me; broken and flawed. A partner who has grown with me through all the heartache and pain and chose never to let go, rather, to hold on tighter. A great house in a great neighborhood that we can build together as a family as we grow. Realizing that some of the new and shiny elements that I desired don't hold a candle to the stories and memories that childhoods and families thrive on. Rather, I am raising the next generation on resiliency and reflection through our stories versus hiding behind them.

I stopped being the master of Shapeshifting. I allowed myself to be still and be seen, fully and completely. I stopped running and allowed myself to be okay with being me. I didn't know how to start the process, but I noticed the first shift happened when I put myself first and started taking the masks off one by one. All of the external roles, the archetypes I identified myself as: grad student, professional, wife, mother, philanthropist, and caregiver. I maxed out my credit card and signed up for an online course to learn how to own your story. For the first time in my life, I decided I was worth the investment to better myself. That course changed my trajectory. Besides therapy, I finally found a solstice in unbecoming everything I told myself I had to be.

I let go of the "comparisonitis" that I was plagued with. I viewed what everyone else had as something I did not which put a strain on my heart and my marriage. It became a spreadable disease that plagued me. I got hot and itchy all over as soon as it flared. Nothing was good enough. Compared to others, I thought we drove shit vehicles, lived in an old, rundown rambler. Although we had degrees and jobs and lived comfortably, it was never enough. We didn't have extra to go on family vacations, they boys weren't in enough activities, and Aaron and I never got to see each other. I questioned what the point to all of this was. Now, I can appreciate building our life on our terms and seeking gratitude in the simple things, because I have found the simple things are what leave imprints on our hearts.

I became present. I was too focused living in past or future, and since most of the time I avoided anything to do with my past, I solely focused on the future. Someday became my mantra, which didn't help anything. I was living for someday versus living for today. It wasn't until I realized that until I viewed my life and myself as good enough, nothing would ever be good enough. That shift of appreciation for the present moment changed everything. The act of appreciation opened my eyes to the little, everyday moments that make my life beautiful.

I practiced gratitude. From the moment I started my gratitude journal eight days after my accident, I reflected on the beauty in the moments that made up the day. Now I choose to appreciate the beauty in the present moment. Not in the morning, not from yesterday, but in the here and now. Being still. Noticing all five of my senses firing. Opening up and going within. Appreciating life at this exact moment.

I set healthy boundaries. I removed toxic people and relationships from my life and my timeline. I didn't need to follow shitty people spreading their shitty attitude everywhere; in person or online. Just by removing those triggers from my life made me much more present and less anxious to keep up with what I do or don't have. Saying yes to me and no to things that do not serve me, or my family has created a positive shift in maintaining balance and healthy family dynamic instead of stretched and drained.

GROWING WILD

READING GUIDE

....

1. At the end of the first chapter, Kathryn questions if she is too much, as that was a recurring theme in her young life. Is there a time where you felt like you've been too much? How did that make an impact on your behavior or demeanor?

2. Healing was a long and hard process for Kathryn. Physically, doctors cleared her. Emotionally, however, was another story. She talks about a soul fracture with the news of Nathan's baby and the betrayal she felt. Where has betrayal shown up in your life? What lessons did you learn or are still learning?

3. Mark's death rocked Kathryn to the core, especially so quickly after Nathan's death. Questions arose of where she belonged, what her purpose was, and how these tragedies were not going to define her. What elements in your life have you used as pivotal moments versus defining moments?

4. We all have a rock bottom moment. The loss of a job, a diagnosis, an addiction, the loss of a loved one. Kathryn found herself at a rock bottom in a jail cell where the all too familiar voice of unworthiness screamed within her head. What brought you to your rock bottom? What did you find out about yourself there?

5. After years of chasing after degrees, titles, and wearing many different masks, Kathryn finally feels like she has made it professionally. However, shame creeps back into the many facets of her world personally through motherhood and obsessing on how things should have been. How did this white picket fence fantasy

coupled with back to back pregnancies and unresolved anger spiral into the perfect storm?

6. At the end of the chapter, Kathryn finds herself in her bathroom where the layers of wallpaper were a direct reflection of the deep transformation that was going on inside of her. What has been a time in your life where the physical world mimicked your internal world?

7. A spiritual journey has begun for Kathryn, following the Speaker Summit where she received confirmation that she was on the right path. Synchronicity followed in her conversations, therapy sessions, and dreams. Has there been a time where by being open to the possibilities, layers of healing have occurred for you?

8. Notice how once Kathryn opened herself up to sharing her story and standing in her strengths, opportunities arose. When in your life have there been moments of alignment by letting go of control?

9. Kathryn found a freedom and solstice by following her heart and flying solo to Bali. It was there that she truly showed up as herself authentically, leaving all the masks behind her. Her relationship with Kat proved to be monumental in uncovering those truths. Who or what in your life has created a soulful impact that changed the trajectory of your life?

10. At the end of the book, Kathryn finds herself back at the Mighty Oak twenty years later, only this time it looked much different than when she was a young girl. What did she find in that tree? What did the tree represent all along?

Additional Questions to Consider:

- Why do you think the author wanted to share his or her story?
- If you were already familiar with the author, has the book changed your view of them?
- Was there anything especially surprising about the author's story?
- Were there any parts of the book where you would have liked more information?
- Did the book remind you of any other memoirs or biographies you've read?
- What did you particularly like or dislike about the book?
- Is the author someone you would want to know?
- Was there a lesson for modern readers could be taken away from the author's life?
- What three words would you use to best describe this book?
- If this was a book that will stay with you awhile, why?

ACKNOWLEDGEMENTS

....

Aaron: My rock, my everything. Thank you for growing wild with me and never letting go.

To my boys, James, Drew, and Jack: You three are my whole heart. I am so proud of all that you are and all that you are growing into being. I love you and every day I thank God that you chose me. James, you made me. Drew, you healed me. Jack, you completed me.

To my parents: Thank you for the gift of eternal, unconditional love and grace. I know I can give more because you demonstrated it, time and time again. You were my first teachers and helped me grow into the person I am today.

Renée: Thank you for answering the call and showing me how to rise up. Each one of my milestones has your imprint on my heart.

Michelle: God placed you in my life at the most perfect time. You showed me what it's like to live and wear my heart on my sleeve unapologetically and to continue to look for the deeper meaning.

Alisia: If it weren't for your guidance and inspiration, there would be no story. Your undeniable belief in me and my story helped me uncover so many truths and heal through my own words. You truly know how to make lead into gold. Thank you for your magic.

To my LadyTribe: Thank you for being a constant. In guidance, in holding space, in unending belief. From growing up together to growing families together. From the coffee dates to the late night texts. You all raise me higher.

To my readers: I am humbled that you walked with me through this journey and I hope that you have found these words helpful in yours. To reopen past hurts and relive some of the most heart wrenching aspects of my life was hard, yet completely cathartic. I am holding space for you as you peel off some of the layers that no longer serve you as you journey through this space.

My open-ended prayer for you is to keep moving forward. Life is a continuum and our lessons keep showing up until we sit and breathe into the uncomfortableness long enough to know that we will rise on the other side. May you know that you are not too much, rather that you are more than enough. May you know that it's okay to rise up while being rooted in your beliefs. And lastly, may you know that growing wild is exactly where you need to be on your journey.

I would love to continue this conversation with you! Please feel free to visit my website at www.kathrynvigness.com for more information on how to book me as a speaker for your next event or to enlist in private coaching with me. For more of my everyday shenanigans, be sure to follow me on Facebook, Instagram, and Twitter.

ABOUT THE AUTHOR

....

Kathryn Vigness is a speaker, author, and life coach. She is a #boymama, yogi, and lover of all things happy. As an avid writer, Kathryn is a featured contributor to multiple online journals and is the author of her memoir Growing Wild and the inspirational journal #soulprompt. Kathryn's only goal at the end of her life is to have lived a life serving others. She is a fireproof change agent and a resiliency advocate. She is living proof that life gives us what we always need, not always we've envisioned. Keep up with Kathryn on Instagram or Facebook at @kvigness or find her at kathrynvigness.com

CPSIA information can be obtained
at www.ICGtesting.com
Printed in the USA
BVHW072142271118
534175BV00003B/300/P

9 780692 175521